MUNITORUM
MANUAL 20...

POINTS VALUES FOR WARHAMMER 40,000

Welcome to the 2021 Mk II edition of the Munitorum Field Manual. This book contains the most up-to-date points values that should be used in your matched play games, covering all the factions in Warhammer 40,000.

To work alongside the Chapter Approved: Grand Tournament 2021 mission pack, we have reviewed all our points values and, where necessary, updated certain unit and wargear costs.

You can use this book to determine the points (pts) value of each unit in your army. Each entry lists the unit's size (i.e. how many models the unit can contain) and how many points the unit costs. If an entry has a unit cost of 'x pts/model', then the unit costs x points for every model in that unit. You must then add the points for each weapon and other item of wargear included in that unit if it is listed in that unit's entry (weapons and other wargear not listed in a unit's entry cost no additional points to include in that unit).

The points values listed in this book replace any published previously, and should be used in your matched play games (or any of your games that are using points values). As with the previous edition of the Munitorum Field Manual, this book contains the points values for every single unit that, at the time of printing, is supported for matched play games, eliminating the need to flip back and forth between two or more books.

We wish you luck on the battlefield.

- Robin Cruddace and the Warhammer 40,000 Rules Team

CONTENTS

PRODUCED BY THE WARHAMMER STUDIO

With thanks to the Mournival and the operatives of the Officio Assassinorum for their additional playtesting services

SPACE MARINES

HQ

Captain

Unit size .... 1 model
Unit cost .... 85 pts
- Combi-flamer .... +5 pts
- Combi-grav .... +5 pts
- Combi-melta .... +5 pts
- Combi-plasma .... +5 pts
- Jump pack .... +25 pts
- Lightning claw (single/pair)* .... +5 pts
- Power axe .... +5 pts
- Power fist .... +10 pts
- Power maul .... +5 pts
- Power sword .... +5 pts
- Relic blade .... +10 pts
- Storm shield .... +10 pts
- Thunder hammer .... +20 pts
- Xenophase blade .... +10 pts

*It is the same points cost to take a single
lightning claw or a pair of lightning claws on
this model.*

Captain in Gravis Armour

Unit size .... 1 model
Unit cost .... 115 pts

Captain in Phobos Armour

Unit size .... 1 model
Unit cost .... 95 pts

Captain in Terminator Armour

Unit size .... 1 model
Unit cost .... 100 pts
- Chainfist .... +5 pts
- Combi-flamer .... +5 pts
- Combi-grav .... +5 pts
- Combi-melta .... +5 pts
- Combi-plasma .... +5 pts
- Power fist .... +5 pts
- Relic blade .... +5 pts
- Storm shield .... +5 pts
- Thunder hammer .... +15 pts
- Wrist-mounted grenade launcher ... +5 pts

Captain on Bike

Unit size .... 1 model
Unit cost .... 100 pts
- Combi-flamer .... +10 pts
- Combi-grav .... +10 pts
- Combi-melta .... +10 pts
- Combi-plasma .... +10 pts
- Grav-pistol .... +5 pts
- Hand flamer .... +5 pts
- Inferno pistol .... +5 pts
- Lightning claw .... +5 pts
- Master-crafted boltgun .... +5 pts
- Plasma pistol .... +5 pts
- Power axe .... +5 pts
- Power fist .... +10 pts
- Power maul .... +5 pts
- Power sword .... + 5 pts
- Storm bolter .... +5 pts
- Storm shield .... +10 pts
- Thunder hammer .... +20 pts

Captain with Master-crafted Heavy Bolt Rifle

Unit size .... 1 model
Unit cost .... 105 pts

Chaplain

Unit size .... 1 model
Unit cost .... 80 pts
- Combi-flamer .... +10 pts
- Combi-grav .... +10 pts
- Combi-melta .... +10 pts
- Combi-plasma .... +10 pts
- Grav-pistol .... +5 pts
- Hand flamer .... +5 pts
- Inferno pistol .... +5 pts
- Jump pack .... +25 pts
- Plasma pistol .... +5 pts
- Power fist .... +10 pts
- Storm bolter .... +5 pts

Chaplain in Terminator Armour

Unit size .... 1 model
Unit cost .... 95 pts
- Combi-flamer .... +5 pts
- Combi-grav .... +5 pts
- Combi-melta .... +5 pts
- Combi-plasma .... +5 pts

Chapter Command

Chapter Ancient .... +20 pts
Chapter Champion .... +15 pts
Chapter Master .... +40 pts
Chief Apothecary .... +35 pts
Chief Librarian .... +25 pts
Master of Sanctity .... +25 pts
Master of the Forge .... +20 pts

Librarian

Unit size .... 1 model
Unit cost .... 90 pts
- Combi-flamer .... +10 pts
- Combi-grav .... +10 pts
- Combi-melta .... +10 pts
- Combi-plasma .... +10 pts
- Grav-pistol .... +5 pts
- Hand flamer .... +5 pts
- Inferno pistol .... +5 pts
- Jump pack .... +25 pts
- Plasma pistol .... +5 pts
- Storm bolter .... +5 pts

Librarian in Phobos Armour

Unit size .... 1 model
Unit cost .... 100 pts

Librarian in Terminator Armour

Unit size .... 1 model
Unit cost .... 105 pts
- Combi-flamer .... +10 pts
- Combi-grav .... +10 pts
- Combi-melta .... +10 pts
- Combi-plasma .... +10 pts
- Storm bolter .... +5 pts

Lieutenant

Unit size .... 1 model
Unit cost .... 70 pts
- Combi-flamer .... +5 pts
- Combi-grav .... +5 pts
- Combi-melta .... +5 pts
- Combi-plasma .... +5 pts
- Jump pack .... +25 pts
- Lightning claw [single/pair]* .... +5 pts
- Power axe .... +5 pts
- Power fist .... +10 pts
- Power maul .... +5 pts
- Power sword .... +5 pts
- Thunder hammer .... +20 pts

*It is the same points cost to take a single
lightning claw or a pair of lightning claws on
this model.*

Lieutenant in Phobos Armour

Unit size .... 1 model
Unit cost .... 80 pts

Lieutenant in Reiver Armour

Unit size .... 1 model
Unit cost .... 75 pts

Primaris Captain
Unit size .... 1 model
Unit cost .... 90 pts
- Master-crafted power sword .... +5 pts
- Power fist .... +10 pts
- Relic shield .... +10 pts

Primaris Chaplain
Unit size .... 1 model
Unit cost .... 85 pts

Primaris Chaplain on Bike
Unit size .... 1 model
Unit cost .... 115 pts

Primaris Librarian
Unit size .... 1 model
Unit cost .... 95 pts

Primaris Lieutenant
Unit size .... 1 model
Unit cost .... 75 pts
- Master-crafted power axe .... +5 pts
- Neo-volkite pistol .... +15 pts
- Plasma pistol .... +5 pts

Primaris Techmarine
Unit size .... 1 model
Unit cost .... 80 pts

Techmarine
Unit size .... 1 model
Unit cost .... 70 pts
- Combi-flamer .... +10 pts
- Combi-grav .... +10 pts
- Combi-melta .... +10 pts
- Combi-plasma .... +10 pts
- Grav-pistol .... +5 pts
- Hand flamer .... +5 pts
- Inferno pistol .... +5 pts
- Plasma cutter .... +15 pts
- Plasma pistol .... +5 pts
- Power fist .... +5 pts
- Storm bolter .... +5 pts
- Tempest hammer .... +20 pts
- Thunder hammer .... +15 pts

TROOPS

Assault Intercessor Squad
Unit size .... 5-10 models
Unit cost .... 19 pts/model
- Hand flamer .... +5 pts
- Plasma pistol .... +5 pts
- Power fist .... +10 pts
- Power sword .... +5 pts
- Thunder hammer .... +20 pts

Heavy Intercessor Squad
Unit size .... 5-10 models
Unit cost .... 28 pts/model
- Executor heavy bolter .... +10 pts
- Heavy bolter .... +10 pts
- Hellstorm heavy bolter .... +10 pts

Incursor Squad
Unit size .... 5-10 models
Unit cost .... 21 pts/model
- Haywire mine .... +10 pts

Infiltrator Squad
Unit size .... 5-10 models
Unit cost .... 24 pts/model
- Helix gauntlet .... +10 pts
- Infiltrator comms array .... +5 pts

Intercessor Squad
Unit size .... 5-10 models
Unit cost .... 20 pts/model
- Astartes grenade launcher .... +5 pts
- Hand flamer .... +5 pts
- Plasma pistol .... +5 pts
- Power fist .... +10 pts
- Power sword .... +5 pts
- Thunder hammer .... +20 pts

Tactical Squad
Unit size .... 5-10 models
Unit cost .... 18 pts/model
- Combi-flamer .... +10 pts
- Combi-grav .... +10 pts
- Combi-melta .... +10 pts
- Combi-plasma .... +10 pts
- Flamer .... +5 pts
- Grav-cannon .... +10 pts
- Grav-gun .... +10 pts
- Grav-pistol .... +5 pts
- Hand flamer .... +5 pts
- Heavy bolter .... +10 pts
- Heavy flamer .... +10 pts
- Inferno pistol .... +5 pts
- Lascannon .... +15 pts
- Lightning claw .... +5 pts
- Meltagun .... +10 pts
- Missile launcher .... +15 pts
- Multi-melta .... +20 pts
- Plasma cannon .... +15 pts
- Plasma gun .... +10 pts
- Plasma pistol .... +5 pts
- Power axe .... +5 pts
- Power fist .... +10 pts
- Power maul .... +5 pts
- Power sword .... +5 pts
- Storm bolter .... +5 pts
- Thunder hammer .... +15 pts

ELITES

Aggressor Squad
Unit size .... 3-6 models
Unit cost .... 40 pts/model
- Fragstorm grenade launcher .... +5 pts

Ancient in Terminator Armour
Unit size .... 1 model
Unit cost .... 100 pts
- Storm shield .... +10 pts
- Thunder hammer .... +10 pts

Apothecary
Unit size .... 1 model
Unit cost .... 75 pts

Bladeguard Ancient
Unit size .... 1 model
Unit cost .... 85 pts

Bladeguard Veteran Squad
Unit size .... 3-6 models
Unit cost .... 35 pts/model
- Neo-volkite pistol .... +5 pts
- Plasma pistol .... +5 pts

Centurion Assault Squad
Unit size .... 3-6 models
Unit cost .... 55 pts/model
- Hurricane bolter .... +10 pts
- Meltagun .... +5 pts

Company Ancient
Unit size .... 1 model
Unit cost .... 75 pts
- Combi-flamer .... +10 pts
- Combi-grav .... +10 pts
- Combi-melta .... +10 pts
- Combi-plasma .... +10 pts
- Grav-pistol .... +5 pts
- Hand flamer .... +5 pts
- Inferno pistol .... +5 pts
- Lightning claw .... +5 pts
- Plasma pistol .... +5 pts
- Power axe .... +5 pts
- Power fist .... +10 pts
- Power maul .... +5 pts
- Power sword .... +5 pts
- Storm bolter .... +5 pts
- Thunder hammer .... +20 pts

Company Champion
Unit size .... 1 model
Unit cost .... 55 pts

Company Veterans
Unit size .... 2-5 models
Unit cost .... 20 pts/model
- Combat shield .... +3 pts
- Combi-flamer .... +10 pts
- Combi-grav .... +10 pts
- Combi-melta .... +10 pts
- Combi-plasma .... +10 pts
- Flamer .... +5 pts
- Grav-cannon .... +10 pts
- Grav-gun .... +10 pts
- Grav-pistol .... +5 pts
- Hand flamer .... +5 pts
- Heavy bolter .... +10 pts
- Heavy flamer .... +10 pts
- Inferno pistol .... +5 pts
- Lascannon .... +15 pts
- Lightning claw .... +3 pts
- Meltagun .... +10 pts
- Missile launcher .... +15 pts
- Multi-melta .... +20 pts
- Plasma cannon .... +15 pts
- Plasma gun .... +10 pts
- Plasma pistol .... +5 pts
- Power axe .... +3 pts
- Power fist .... +8 pts
- Power maul .... +3 pts
- Power sword .... +3 pts
- Storm bolter .... +5 pts
- Storm shield .... +4 pts
- Thunder hammer .... +12 pts

Contemptor Dreadnought
Unit size ....1 model
Unit cost ....150 pts

Dreadnought
Unit size ....1 model
Unit cost ....120 pts
- Heavy flamer......................................+5 pts
- Helfrost cannon..................................+5 pts
- Multi-melta...+5 pts
- Twin lascannon.................................+20 pts

Invictor Tactical Warsuit
Unit size ....1 model
Unit cost ....160 pts

Ironclad Dreadnought
Unit size ....1 model
Unit cost ....135 pts
- Heavy flamer......................................+5 pts
- Hunter-killer missile ....+5 pts
- Hurricane bolter ....+5 pts
- Ironclad assault launchers ....+5 pts

Judiciar
Unit size ....1 model
Unit cost ....85 pts

Primaris Apothecary
Unit size ....1 model
Unit cost ....80 pts

Primaris Ancient
Unit size ....1 model
Unit cost ....80 pts

Redemptor Dreadnought
Unit size ....1 model
Unit cost ....175 pts
- Icarus rocket pod ....+5 pts
- Onslaught gatling cannon ....+5 pts

Reiver Squad
Unit size ....5-10 models
Unit cost ....18 pts/model
- Grapnel launcher ....+2 pts
- Reiver grav-chute.............................+2 pts

Relic Terminator Squad
Unit size ....5-10 models
Unit cost ....34 pts/model
- Chainfist...+5 pts
- Grenade harness ....+5 pts
- Heavy flamer......................................+5 pts
- Plasma blaster....................................+5 pts
- Power fist..+5 pts
- Reaper autocannon...........................+5 pts
- Volkite charger...................................+5 pts

Scout Squad
Unit size ....5-10 models
Unit cost ....14 pts/model
- Camo cloak ....+2 pts
- Combi-flamer.....................................+10 pts
- Combi-grav...+10 pts
- Combi-melta.......................................+10 pts
- Combi-plasma....................................+10 pts
- Flamer..+5 pts
- Grav-gun...+5 pts
- Grav-pistol..+5 pts
- Hand flamer..+5 pts
- Heavy bolter......................................+10 pts
- Inferno pistol.....................................+5 pts
- Lightning claw ....+5 pts
- Meltagun ....+10 pts
- Missile launcher ....+15 pts
- Plasma gun ....+10 pts
- Plasma pistol ....+5 pts
- Power axe ....+5 pts
- Power fist ....+10 pts
- Power maul..+5 pts
- Power sword ....+5 pts
- Scout sniper rifle ....+2 pts
- Storm bolter ....+5 pts
- Thunder hammer ....+15 pts

Servitors
Unit size .... 4 models
Unit cost ....30 pts
- Heavy bolter.......................................+5 pts
- Multi-melta.......................................+15 pts
- Plasma cannon..................................+10 pts

Sternguard Veteran Squad
Unit size ....5-10 models
Unit cost ....20 pts/model
- Combi-flamer.....................................+5 pts
- Combi-grav...+5 pts
- Combi-melta.......................................+5 pts
- Combi-plasma....................................+5 pts
- Flamer..+5 pts
- Grav-cannon.....................................+10 pts
- Grav-gun...+10 pts
- Grav-pistol..+5 pts
- Hand flamer..+5 pts
- Heavy bolter......................................+10 pts
- Heavy flamer....................................+10 pts
- Inferno pistol.....................................+5 pts
- Lascannon...+15 pts
- Lightning claw ....+5 pts
- Meltagun ....+10 pts
- Missile launcher ....+15 pts
- Multi-melta.......................................+20 pts
- Plasma cannon.................................+15 pts
- Plasma gun ....+10 pts
- Plasma pistol ....+5 pts
- Power axe ....+5 pts
- Power fist ....+10 pts
- Power maul..+5 pts
- Power sword ....+5 pts
- Storm bolter ....+3 pts

Terminator Assault Squad
Unit size ....5-10 models
Unit cost ....33 pts/model
- Teleport homer ....+5 pts
- Thunder hammer ....+10 pts

Terminator Squad
Unit size ....5-10 models
Unit cost ....38 pts/model
- Assault cannon ....+10 pts
- Cyclone missile launcher................+25 pts
- Heavy flamer......................................+5 pts
- Teleport homer ....+5 pts

Vanguard Veteran Squad
Unit size ....5-10 models
Unit cost ....19 pts/model
- Grav-pistol..+5 pts
- Hand flamer..+5 pts
- Heavy thunder hammer...................+15 pts
- Inferno pistol.....................................+5 pts
- Jump pack ....+3 pts
- Lightning claw ....+3 pts
- Plasma pistol ....+5 pts
- Power axe ....+3 pts
- Power fist ....+8 pts
- Power maul..+3 pts
- Power sword ....+3 pts
- Relic blade ....+10 pts
- Storm shield ....+5 pts
- Thunder hammer ....+12 pts

Venerable Dreadnought
Unit size ....1 model
Unit cost ....135 pts
- Blizzard shield ....+15 pts
- Fenrisian great axe ....+10 pts
- Heavy flamer......................................+5 pts
- Helfrost cannon..................................+5 pts
- Multi-melta...+5 pts
- Twin lascannon.................................+20 pts

Veteran Intercessor Squad
Unit size ....5-10 models
Unit cost ....22 pts/model
- Astartes grenade launcher ....+5 pts
- Hand flamer..+5 pts
- Plasma pistol ....+5 pts
- Power fist ....+10 pts
- Power sword ....+5 pts
- Thunder hammer ....+20 pts

FAST ATTACK

Assault Squad
Unit size ....5-10 models
Unit cost ....18 pts/model
- Combat shield....................................+5 pts
- Eviscerator ....+10 pts
- Flamer..+5 pts
- Grav-pistol..+5 pts
- Hand flamer..+5 pts
- Inferno pistol.....................................+5 pts
- Jump pack ....+2 pts
- Lightning claw ....+5 pts
- Meltagun ....+10 pts
- Plasma pistol ....+5 pts
- Plasma gun ....+10 pts
- Power axe ....+5 pts
- Power fist ....+10 pts
- Power maul..+5 pts
- Power sword ....+5 pts
- Thunder hammer ....+15 pts

Attack Bike Squad
Unit size..1-3 models
Unit cost..50 pts/model
- Multi-melta ....+10 pts

Bike Squad
Unit size..3-9 models*
Unit cost..30 pts/model
- Combi-flamer..+10 pts
- Combi-grav..+10 pts
- Combi-melta..+10 pts
- Combi-plasma...+10 pts
- Flamer..+5 pts
- Grav-gun..+10 pts
- Grav-pistol...+5 pts
- Hand flamer...+5 pts
- Heavy bolter..+20 pts
- Inferno pistol...+5 pts
- Lightning claw..+5 pts
- Meltagun..+10 pts
- Multi-melta ....+30 pts
- Plasma gun..+10 pts
- Plasma pistol..+5 pts
- Power axe...+5 pts
- Power fist...+10 pts
- Power maul...+5 pts
- Power sword...+5 pts
- Storm bolter...+5 pts
- Thunder hammer......................................+15 pts

If Space Wolves (one of its successor Chapters), unit size is 3-16.

Inceptor Squad
Unit size..3-6 models
Unit cost..40 pts/model
- Plasma exterminator ....+10 pts

Invader ATV Squad
Unit size..1-3 models
Unit cost..80 pts/model
- Multi-melta ....+5 pts

Land Speeders
Unit size..1-3 models
Unit cost..60 pts/model
- Multi-melta ....+10 pts

Land Speeder Tornadoes
Unit size..1-3 models
Unit cost..75 pts/model
- Assault cannon..+5 pts
- Multi-melta ....+10 pts

Land Speeder Typhoons
Unit size..1-3 models
Unit cost..110 pts/model
- Multi-melta ....+10 pts

Outrider Squad
Unit size..3 models
Unit cost..50 pts/model

Scout Bike Squad
Unit size..3-9 models
Unit cost..30 pts/model
- Combi-flamer..+10 pts
- Combi-grav..+10 pts
- Combi-melta..+10 pts
- Combi-plasma...+10 pts
- Grav-pistol...+5 pts
- Hand flamer...+5 pts
- Inferno pistol...+5 pts
- Lightning claw..+5 pts
- Plasma pistol..+5 pts
- Power axe...+5 pts
- Power fist...+10 pts
- Power maul...+5 pts
- Power sword...+5 pts
- Storm bolter...+5 pts
- Thunder hammer......................................+15 pts

Storm Speeder Hailstrike
Unit size..1 model
Unit cost..135 pts/model

Storm Speeder Hammerstrike
Unit size..1 model
Unit cost..155 pts/model

Storm Speeder Thunderstrike
Unit size..1 model
Unit cost..160 pts/model

Suppressor Squad
Unit size..3 models
Unit cost..100 pts

HEAVY SUPPORT

Centurion Devastator Squad
Unit size..3-6 models
Unit cost..70 pts/model
- Grav-cannon...+15 pts
- Heavy bolter..+15 pts
- Lascannon...+20 pts

Devastator Squad
Unit size..5-10 models
Unit cost..18 pts/model
- Armorium cherub....................................+5 pts
- Combi-flamer..+10 pts
- Combi-grav..+10 pts
- Combi-melta..+10 pts
- Combi-plasma...+10 pts
- Grav-cannon...+10 pts
- Grav-pistol...+5 pts
- Hand flamer...+5 pts
- Heavy bolter..+10 pts
- Heavy flamer..+10 pts
- Inferno pistol...+5 pts
- Lascannon...+15 pts
- Lightning claw..+5 pts
- Missile launcher.......................................+15 pts
- Multi-melta ....+20 pts
- Plasma cannon..+15 pts
- Plasma pistol..+5 pts
- Power axe...+5 pts
- Power fist...+10 pts
- Power maul...+5 pts
- Power sword...+5 pts
- Storm bolter...+5 pts
- Thunder hammer......................................+15 pts

Eliminator Squad
Unit size..3 models
Unit cost..25 pts/model
- Las fusil...+5 pts

Eradicator Squad
Unit size..3-6 models
Unit cost..45 pts/model
- Heavy melta rifle......................................+5 pts
- Multi-melta ....+10 pts

Firestrike Servo-turrets
Unit size..1-3 models
Unit cost..90 pts/model
- Twin las-talon..+40 pts

Gladiator Lancer
Unit size..1 model
Unit cost..180 pts
- Auto launchers..+5 pts
- Icarus rocket pod.....................................+5 pts
- Ironhail heavy stubber.............................+5 pts

Gladiator Reaper
Unit size..1 model
Unit cost..210 pts
- Auto launchers..+5 pts
- Icarus rocket pod.....................................+5 pts
- Ironhail heavy stubber.............................+5 pts

Gladiator Valiant
Unit size..1 model
Unit cost..230 pts
- Auto launchers..+5 pts
- Icarus rocket pod.....................................+5 pts
- Ironhail heavy stubber.............................+5 pts

Hellblaster Squad
Unit size..5-10 models
Unit cost..33 pts/model
- Plasma pistol..+5 pts

Hunter
Unit size..1 model
Unit cost..110 pts
- Hunter-killer missile.................................+5 pts
- Storm bolter...+5 pts

Land Raider
Unit size..1 model
Unit cost..265 pts
- Hunter-killer missile.................................+5 pts
- Multi-melta ....+25 pts
- Storm bolter...+5 pts

Land Raider Crusader
Unit size..1 model
Unit cost..265 pts
- Hunter-killer missile.................................+5 pts
- Multi-melta ....+25 pts
- Storm bolter...+5 pts

Land Raider Redeemer
Unit size..1 model
Unit cost..265 pts
- Hunter-killer missile ....+5 pts
- Multi-melta ....+25 pts
- Storm bolter...+5 pts

Predator Annihilator

Unit size	1 model
Unit cost	130 pts
• Heavy bolter	+15 pts
• Hunter-killer missile	+5 pts
• Lascannon	+20 pts
• Storm bolter	+5 pts

Predator Destructor

Unit size	1 model
Unit cost	140 pts
• Heavy bolter	+15 pts
• Hunter-killer missile	+5 pts
• Lascannon	+20 pts
• Storm bolter	+5 pts

Repulsor

Unit size	1 model
Unit cost	295 pts
• Las-talon	+5 pts
• Onslaught gatling cannon	+15 pts
• Twin lascannon	+10 pts

Repulsor Executioner

Unit size	1 model
Unit cost	335 pts
• Heavy laser destructor	+10 pts
• Icarus rocket pod	+5 pts
• Ironhail heavy stubber	+5 pts

Stalker

Unit size	1 model
Unit cost	115 pts
• Hunter-killer missile	+5 pts
• Storm bolter	+5 pts

Thunderfire Cannon

Unit size	2 models (1 Gunner, 1 Artillery)
Unit cost	120 pts

Vindicator

Unit size	1 model
Unit cost	130 pts
• Hunter-killer missile	+5 pts
• Storm bolter	+5 pts
• Vindicator siege shield	+10 pts

Whirlwind

Unit size	1 model
Unit cost	125 pts
• Hunter-killer missile	+5 pts
• Storm bolter	+5 pts
• Whirlwind vengeance launcher	+10 pts

DEDICATED TRANSPORTS

Drop Pod

Unit size	1 model
Unit cost	70 pts

Impulsor

Unit size	1 model
Unit cost	110 pts
• Bellicatus missile array	+20 pts
• Ironhail heavy stubber	+5 pts
• Ironhail skytalon array	+10 pts
• Orbital comms array	+15 pts
• Shield dome	+15 pts

Land Speeder Storm

Unit size	1 model
Unit cost	55 pts

Razorback

Unit size	1 model
Unit cost	110 pts
• Hunter-killer missile	+5 pts
• Storm bolter	+5 pts
• Twin assault cannon	+15 pts
• Twin lascannon	+10 pts

Rhino

Unit size	1 model
Unit cost	80 pts
• Additional storm bolter	+5 pts
• Hunter-killer missile	+5 pts

FLYERS

Stormhawk Interceptor

Unit size	1 model
Unit cost	185 pts
• Heavy bolter	+5 pts
• Las-talon	+25 pts
• Typhoon missile launcher	+20 pts

Stormraven Gunship

Unit size	1 model
Unit cost	290 pts
• Hurricane bolter	+15 pts
• Twin lascannon	+10 pts
• Twin multi-melta	+20 pts
• Typhoon missile launcher	+10 pts

Stormtalon Gunship

Unit size	1 model
Unit cost	165 pts
• Heavy bolter	+5 pts
• Lascannon	+10 pts
• Typhoon missile launcher	+20 pts

FORTIFICATIONS

Hammerfall Bunker

Unit size	1 model
Unit cost	175 pts

ULTRAMARINES

HQ

Captain Sicarius

Unit size	1 model
Unit cost	115 pts

Chaplain Cassius

Unit size	1 model
Unit cost	95 pts

Chief Librarian Tigurius

Unit size	1 model
Unit cost	135 pts

Marneus Calgar

Unit size	1 model
Unit cost	210 pts

Sergeant Chronus

Unit size	1 model
Unit cost	35 pts

Sergeant Telion

Unit size	1 model
Unit cost	70 pts

Uriel Ventris

Unit size	1 model
Unit cost	110 pts

ELITES

Chapter Ancient

Unit size	1 model
Unit cost	100 pts

Chapter Champion

Unit size	1 model
Unit cost	75 pts

Honour Guard

Unit size	2 models
Unit cost	25 pts/model

Tyrannic War Veterans

Unit size	4-10 models
Unit cost	17 pts/model

Victrix Honour Guard

Unit size	2 models
Unit cost	35 pts/model

LORDS OF WAR

Roboute Guilliman

Unit size	1 model
Unit cost	380 pts

WHITE SCARS

HQ

Khan on Bike
Unit size ....1 model
Unit cost .... 110 pts

Kor'sarro Khan
Unit size ....1 model
Unit cost .... 110 pts

IRON HANDS

HQ

Iron Father Feirros
Unit size ....1 model
Unit cost .... 160 pts

IMPERIAL FISTS

HQ

Captain Lysander
Unit size ....1 model
Unit cost .... 140 pts

Pedro Kantor
Unit size ....1 model
Unit cost .... 155 pts

Tor Garadon
Unit size ....1 model
Unit cost .... 145 pts

SALAMANDERS

HQ

Adrax Agatone
Unit size ....1 model
Unit cost .... 145 pts

Vulkan He'stan
Unit size ....1 model
Unit cost .... 135 pts

BLACK TEMPLARS

HQ

Chaplain Grimaldus
Unit size ....1 model
Unit cost .... 95 pts

The Emperor's Champion
Unit size ....1 model
Unit cost .... 80 pts

High Marshal Helbrecht
Unit size ....1 model
Unit cost .... 155 pts

TROOPS

Crusader Squad
Unit size ....5-20 models
Unit cost (Initiate) ....15 pts/model
Unit cost (Neophyte) ....14 pts/model
- Combi-flamer .... +10 pts
- Combi-grav .... +10 pts
- Combi-melta .... +10 pts
- Combi-plasma .... +10 pts
- Flamer .... +5 pts
- Grav-pistol .... +5 pts
- Grav-cannon .... +10 pts
- Grav-gun .... +10 pts
- Heavy bolter .... +10 pts
- Lascannon .... +15 pts
- Lightning claw .... +5 pts
- Meltagun .... +10 pts
- Missile launcher .... +15 pts
- Multi-melta .... +20 pts
- Plasma cannon .... +15 pts
- Plasma gun .... +10 pts
- Plasma pistol .... +5 pts
- Power axe .... +5 pts
- Power fist .... +10 pts
- Power maul .... +5 pts
- Power sword .... +5 pts
- Storm bolter .... +3 pts
- Thunder hammer .... +15 pts

ELITES

Cenobyte Servitors
Unit size ....3 models
Unit cost .... 6 pts/model

RAVEN GUARD

HQ

Kayvaan Shrike
Unit size .... 1 model
Unit cost .... 135 pts

BLOOD ANGELS

HQ

Astorath
Unit size .... 1 model
Unit cost .... 150 pts

Brother Corbulo
Unit size .... 1 model
Unit cost .... 115 pts

Captain Tycho
Unit size .... 1 model
Unit cost .... 95 pts

Chief Librarian Mephiston
Unit size .... 1 model
Unit cost .... 155 pts

Commander Dante
Unit size .... 1 model
Unit cost .... 165 pts

Gabriel Seth
Unit size .... 1 model
Unit cost .... 160 pts

Lemartes
Unit size .... 1 model
Unit cost .... 120 pts

Librarian Dreadnought
Unit size .... 1 model
Unit cost .... 150 pts
- Heavy flamer .... +5 pts
- Meltagun .... +5 pts

Sanguinary Priest
Unit size .... 1 model
Unit cost .... 90 pts
- Jump pack .... +30 pts

The Sanguinor
Unit size .... 1 model
Unit cost .... 150 pts

Tycho the Lost
Unit size .... 1 model
Unit cost .... 100 pts

ELITES

Death Company Marines
Unit size .... 5-10 models
Unit cost .... 22 pts/model
- Hand flamer .... +5 pts
- Inferno pistol .... +5 pts
- Jump pack .... +3 pts
- Plasma pistol .... +5 pts
- Power axe .... +5 pts
- Power fist .... +10 pts
- Power maul .... +5 pts
- Power sword .... +5 pts
- Thunder hammer .... +15 pts

Death Company Dreadnought
Unit size .... 1 model
Unit cost .... 125 pts
- Blood talons .... +5 pts
- Heavy flamer .... +5 pts
- Magna-grapple .... +5 pts
- Meltagun .... +5 pts

Death Company Intercessors
Unit size .... 5-10 models
Unit cost .... 24 pts/model
- Astartes grenade launcher .... +5 pts
- Hand flamer .... +5 pts
- Plasma pistol .... +5 pts
- Power fist .... +10 pts
- Power sword .... +5 pts
- Thunder hammer .... +20 pts

Furioso Dreadnought
Unit size .... 1 model
Unit cost .... 120 pts
- Blood talons .... +5 pts
- Heavy flamer .... +5 pts
- Magna-grapple .... +5 pts
- Meltagun .... +5 pts

Sanguinary Ancient
Unit size .... 1 model
Unit cost .... 110 pts
- Inferno pistol .... +5 pts
- Plasma pistol .... +5 pts

Sanguinary Guard
Unit size .... 4-10 models
Unit cost .... 32 pts/model
- Inferno pistol .... +5 pts
- Plasma pistol .... +5 pts
- Power fist .... +5 pts

HEAVY SUPPORT

Baal Predator
Unit size .... 1 model
Unit cost .... 120 pts
- Heavy bolter .... +15 pts
- Heavy flamer .... +15 pts
- Hunter-killer missile .... +5 pts
- Storm bolter .... +5 pts
- Twin assault cannon .... +10 pts

'The Lost' Upgrades
CAPTAIN .... +20 pts
LIEUTENANT .... +10 pts

DARK ANGELS

HQ

Asmodai
Unit size...1 model
Unit cost...130 pts

Azrael
Unit size...1 model
Unit cost...170 pts

Belial
Unit size...1 model
Unit cost...140 pts

Ezekiel
Unit size...1 model
Unit cost...125 pts

Interrogator-Chaplain
Unit size...1 model
Unit cost...85 pts
- Combi-flamer ....+5 pts
- Combi-grav.......................................+5 pts
- Combi-melta.....................................+5 pts
- Combi-plasma...................................+5 pts
- Grav-pistol ....+5 pts
- Jump pack ....+25 pts
- Lightning claw ....+5 pts
- Plasma pistol ....+5 pts
- Power axe ....+5 pts
- Power fist ....+10 pts
- Power maul ....+5 pts
- Power sword ....+5 pts
- Storm bolter.....................................+5 pts
- Thunder hammer ....+20 pts

Interrogator-Chaplain in terminator Armour
Unit size...1 model
Unit cost...100 pts
- Combi-flamer .... +5 pts
- Combi-grav.......................................+5 pts
- Combi-melta.....................................+5 pts
- Combi-plasma...................................+5 pts

Lazarus
Unit size...1 model
Unit cost...110 pts

Ravenwing Talonmaster
Unit size...1 model
Unit cost...175 pts

Sammael
Unit size...1 model
Unit cost...150 pts

Deathwing Strikemaster
Unit size...1 model
Unit cost...95 pts
- Chainfist...+5 pts
- Mace of absolution...........................+10 pts
- Storm shield ....+5 pts
- Thunder hammer ....+10 pts

ELITES

Deathwing Apothecary
Unit size...1 model
Unit cost...100 pts

Deathwing Champion
Unit size...1 model
Unit cost...80 pts

Deathwing Command Squad
Unit size................................... 2-5 models
Unit cost....................................35 pts/model
- Assault cannon ....+10 pts
- Chainfist...+5 pts
- Cyclone missile launcher..................+25 pts
- Heavy flamer....................................+5 pts
- Plasma cannon.................................+10 pts
- Power fist ....+5 pts
- Thunder hammer ....+10 pts
- Watcher in the Dark.........................+5 pts

Deathwing Knights
Unit size...............................5-10 models
Unit cost....................................47 pts/model
- Watcher in the Dark.........................+5 pts

Deathwing Terminator Squad
Unit size...............................5-10 models
Unit cost....................................33 pts/model
- Assault cannon ....+10 pts
- Chainfist...+5 pts
- Cyclone missile launcher..................+25 pts
- Heavy flamer....................................+5 pts
- Plasma cannon.................................+10 pts
- Power fist ....+5 pts
- Thunder hammer ....+10 pts
- Watcher in the Dark.........................+5 pts

Ravenwing Ancient
Unit size...1 model
Unit cost...100 pts

Ravenwing Apothecary
Unit size...1 model
Unit cost...100 pts

Ravenwing Black Knights
Unit size...............................3-10 models
Unit cost....................................40 pts/model
- Corvus hammer.................................+5 pts
- Power maul ....+5 pts
- Power sword ....+5 pts

Ravenwing Champion
Unit size...1 model
Unit cost...70 pts

FAST ATTACK

Ravenwing Darkshroud
Unit size...1 model
Unit cost...130 pts
- Assault cannon ....+5 pts

Ravenwing Land Speeder Vengeance
Unit size...1 model
Unit cost...120 pts
- Assault cannon ....+5 pts

FLYERS

Nephilim Jetfighter
Unit size...1 model
Unit cost...190 pts

Ravenwing Dark Talon
Unit size...1 model
Unit cost...210 pts

Rites of Initiation
CAPTAIN...+20 pts
PRIMARIS LIEUTENANT
equipped with storm shield ....+15 pts
DREADNOUGHT.......................................+15 pts
LAND RAIDER...+10 pts
REPULSOR ....+10 pts
STORMRAVEN GUNSHIP.....................+10 pts
TRANSPORT that can
transport TERMINATORS.................+10 pts

SPACE WOLVES

HQ

Arjac Rockfist
Unit size...1 model
Unit cost...120 pts

Bjorn the Fell-Handed
Unit size...1 model
Unit cost...175 pts
- Helfrost cannon................................+5 pts
- Multi-melta......................................+5 pts
- Twin lascannon..............................+20 pts

Canis Wolfborn
Unit size...1 model
Unit cost...120 pts

Harald Deathwolf
Unit size...1 model
Unit cost...140 pts

Krom Dragongaze
Unit size...1 model
Unit cost...100 pts

Logan Grimnar
Unit size...1 model
Unit cost...155 pts

Logan Grimnar on Stormrider
Unit size...1 model
Unit cost...180 pts

Njal Stormcaller
Unit size...1 model
Unit cost...140 pts

Ragnar Blackmane
Unit size...1 model
Unit cost...130 pts

Ulrik the Slayer
Unit size...1 model
Unit cost...110 pts

Wolf Guard Battle Leader in Terminator Armour
Unit size...1 model
Unit cost...85 pts
- Combi-flamer....................................+5 pts
- Combi-grav.......................................+5 pts
- Combi-melta......................................+5 pts
- Combi-plasma....................................+5 pts
- Chainfist...+5 pts
- Power fist..+5 pts
- Storm shield.....................................+5 pts
- Thunder hammer.............................+15 pts

Wolf Guard Battle Leader on Thunderwolf
Unit size...1 model
Unit cost...95 pts
- Combi-flamer..................................+10 pts
- Combi-grav.....................................+10 pts
- Combi-melta....................................+10 pts
- Combi-plasma..................................+10 pts
- Plasma pistol....................................+5 pts
- Lightning claw..................................+5 pts
- Power axe...+5 pts
- Power fist..+10 pts
- Power maul.......................................+5 pts
- Power sword......................................+5 pts
- Storm bolter......................................+5 pts
- Storm shield....................................+10 pts
- Thunder hammer.............................+20 pts

Wolf Lord on Thunderwolf
Unit size...1 model
Unit cost...110 pts
- Combi-flamer..................................+10 pts
- Combi-grav.....................................+10 pts
- Combi-melta....................................+10 pts
- Combi-plasma..................................+10 pts
- Lightning claw..................................+5 pts
- Plasma pistol....................................+5 pts
- Power axe...+5 pts
- Power fist..+10 pts
- Power maul.......................................+5 pts
- Power sword......................................+5 pts
- Storm bolter......................................+5 pts
- Storm shield....................................+10 pts
- Thunder hammer.............................+20 pts

TROOPS

Blood Claws
Unit size.................................5-15 models
Unit cost.................................18 pts/model
- Flamer...+5 pts
- Grav-gun...+5 pts
- Meltagun..+10 pts
- Plasma gun.....................................+10 pts
- Plasma pistol....................................+5 pts
- Power axe...+5 pts
- Power fist..+10 pts
- Power sword......................................+5 pts

This unit can also include one of the following:
Wolf Guard Pack Leader....................+18 pts
- Combi-flamer..................................+10 pts
- Combi-grav.....................................+10 pts
- Combi-melta....................................+10 pts
- Combi-plasma..................................+10 pts
- Lightning claw..................................+5 pts
- Plasma pistol....................................+5 pts
- Power axe...+5 pts
- Power fist..+10 pts
- Power maul.......................................+5 pts
- Power sword......................................+5 pts
- Storm bolter......................................+5 pts
- Storm shield......................................+5 pts
- Thunder hammer.............................+15 pts

Wolf Guard Terminator Pack Leader..........+33 pts
- Combi-flamer....................................+5 pts
- Combi-grav.......................................+5 pts
- Combi-melta......................................+5 pts
- Combi-plasma....................................+5 pts
- Chainfist...+5 pts
- Power fist..+5 pts
- Storm shield.....................................+5 pts
- Thunder hammer.............................+10 pts

Grey Hunters
Unit size.................................5-10 models
Unit cost.................................18 pts/model
- Astartes chainsword...........................+1 pt
- Flamer...+5 pts
- Grav-gun...+5 pts
- Meltagun..+10 pts
- Plasma gun.....................................+10 pts
- Plasma pistol....................................+5 pts
- Power axe...+5 pts
- Power fist..+10 pts
- Power sword......................................+5 pts
- Wolf standard....................................+5 pts

This unit can also include one of the following:
Wolf Guard Pack Leader....................+18 pts
- Astartes chainsword...........................+1 pt
- Combi-flamer..................................+10 pts
- Combi-grav.....................................+10 pts
- Combi-melta....................................+10 pts
- Combi-plasma..................................+10 pts
- Lightning claw..................................+5 pts
- Plasma pistol....................................+5 pts
- Power axe...+5 pts
- Power fist..+10 pts
- Power maul.......................................+5 pts
- Power sword......................................+5 pts
- Storm bolter......................................+5 pts
- Storm shield......................................+5 pts
- Thunder hammer.............................+15 pts

Wolf Guard Terminator Pack Leader..........+33 pts
- Combi-flamer....................................+5 pts
- Combi-grav.......................................+5 pts
- Combi-melta......................................+5 pts
- Combi-plasma....................................+5 pts
- Chainfist...+5 pts
- Power fist..+5 pts
- Storm shield.....................................+5 pts
- Thunder hammer.............................+10 pts

ELITES

Hounds of Morkai
Unit size .... 5-10 models
Unit cost .... 22 pts/model

Lukas the Trickster
Unit size .... 1 model
Unit cost .... 80 pts

Murderfang
Unit size .... 1 model
Unit cost .... 150 pts

Wolf Guard
Unit size .... 5-10 models
Unit cost .... 19 pts/model
- Combi-flamer .... +10 pts
- Combi-grav .... +10 pts
- Combi-melta .... +10 pts
- Combi-plasma .... +10 pts
- Jump pack .... +2 pts
- Lightning claw .... +3 pts
- Plasma pistol .... +5 pts
- Power axe .... +3 pts
- Power fist .... +8 pts
- Power maul .... +3 pts
- Power sword .... +3 pts
- Storm bolter .... +5 pts
- Storm shield .... +4 pts
- Thunder hammer .... +12 pts

Wolf Guard Terminators
Unit size .... 5-10 models
Unit cost .... +33 pts/model
- Assault cannon .... +10 pts
- Chainfist .... +5 pts
- Combi-flamer .... +5 pts
- Combi-grav .... +5 pts
- Combi-melta .... +5 pts
- Combi-plasma .... +5 pts
- Cyclone missile launcher .... +25 pts
- Heavy flamer .... +5 pts
- Power fist .... +5 pts
- Thunder hammer .... +10 pts

Wulfen
Unit size .... 5-10 models
Unit cost .... 22 pts/model
- Great frost axe .... +8 pts
- Stormfrag auto-launcher .... +3 pts
- Thunder hammer .... +16 pts
- Wulfen frost claws .... +5 pts

Wulfen Dreadnought
Unit size .... 1 model
Unit cost .... 120 pts
- Heavy flamer .... +5 pts
- Blizzard shield .... +5 pts

FAST ATTACK

Cyberwolves
Unit size .... 1-5 models
Unit cost .... 15 pts/model

Fenrisian Wolves
Unit size .... 5-15 models
Unit cost .... 7 pts/model

This unit can also include:
Cyberwolf .... +15 pts

Skyclaws
Unit size .... 5-15 models
Unit cost .... 20 pts/model
- Flamer .... +5 pts
- Grav-gun .... +5 pts
- Meltagun .... +10 pts
- Plasma gun .... +10 pts
- Plasma pistol .... +5 pts
- Power axe .... +5 pts
- Power fist .... +10 pts
- Power sword .... +5 pts

This unit can also include:
Wolf Guard Skyclaw Pack Leader ...... +20 pts
- Combi-flamer .... +10 pts
- Combi-grav .... +10 pts
- Combi-melta .... +10 pts
- Combi-plasma .... +10 pts
- Lightning claw .... +5 pts
- Plasma pistol .... +5 pts
- Power axe .... +5 pts
- Power fist .... +10 pts
- Power maul .... +5 pts
- Power sword .... +5 pts
- Storm bolter .... +5 pts
- Storm shield .... +5 pts
- Thunder hammer .... +15 pts

Thunderwolf Cavalry
Unit size .... 3-6 models
Unit cost .... 45 pts/model
- Lightning claw .... +5 pts
- Plasma pistol .... +5 pts
- Power axe .... +5 pts
- Power fist .... +10 pts
- Power maul .... +5 pts
- Power sword .... +5 pts
- Storm shield .... +5 pts
- Thunder hammer .... +15 pts

HEAVY SUPPORT

Long Fangs
Unit size .... 5-6 models
Unit cost .... 18 pts/model
- Armorium Cherub .... +5 pts
- Flamer .... +5 pts
- Grav-cannon .... +10 pts
- Grav-gun .... +5 pts
- Heavy bolter .... +10 pts
- Lascannon .... +15 pts
- Meltagun .... +10 pts
- Missile launcher .... +15 pts
- Multi-melta .... +20 pts
- Plasma cannon .... +15 pts
- Plasma gun .... +10 pts
- Plasma pistol .... +5 pts
- Power axe .... +5 pts
- Power fist .... +10 pts
- Power sword .... +5 pts

This unit can also include one of the following:
Wolf Guard Pack Leader .... +18 pts
- Combi-flamer .... +10 pts
- Combi-grav .... +10 pts
- Combi-melta .... +10 pts
- Combi-plasma .... +10 pts
- Lightning claw .... +5 pts
- Plasma pistol .... +5 pts
- Power axe .... +5 pts
- Power fist .... +10 pts
- Power maul .... +5 pts
- Power sword .... +5 pts
- Storm bolter .... +5 pts
- Storm shield .... +5 pts
- Thunder hammer .... +15 pts

Wolf Guard Terminator Pack Leader .... +33 pts
- Assault cannon .... +5 pts
- Combi-flamer .... +5 pts
- Combi-grav .... +5 pts
- Combi-melta .... +5 pts
- Combi-plasma .... +5 pts
- Chainfist .... +5 pts
- Cyclone missile launcher .... +25 pts
- Heavy flamer .... +5 pts
- Power fist .... +5 pts
- Storm shield .... +5 pts
- Thunder hammer .... +10 pts

FLYERS

Stormfang Gunship
Unit size .... 1 model
Unit cost .... 280 pts
- Lascannon .... +10 pts
- Melta array .... +25 pts
- Twin heavy bolter .... +20 pts

Stormwolf
Unit size .... 1 model
Unit cost .... 280 pts
- Melta array .... +25 pts
- Twin heavy bolter .... +20 pts

DEATHWATCH

HQ

Chaplain Cassius
Unit size .... 1 model
Unit cost .... 95 pts

Codicier Natorian
Unit size .... 1 model
Unit cost .... 100 pts

Watch Captain Artemis
Unit size .... 1 model
Unit cost .... 105 pts

Watch Master
Unit size .... 1 model
Unit cost .... 130 pts

TROOPS

Deathwatch Veterans
Unit size .... 5-10 models
Unit cost (Black Shield) .... 25 pts/model
Unit cost (other models) .... 20 pts/model
- Combat shield .... +4 pts
- Deathwatch combi-flamer .... +5 pts
- Deathwatch combi-grav .... +10 pts
- Deathwatch combi-melta .... +10 pts
- Deathwatch combi-plasma .... +10 pts
- Deathwatch frag cannon .... +10 pts
- Flamer .... +5pts
- Grav-gun .... +5 pts
- Grav-pistol .... +5 pts
- Inferno pistol .... +5 pts
- Infernus heavy bolter .... +15 pts
- Hand flamer .... +5 pts
- Heavy bolter .... +10 pts
- Heavy flamer .... +10 pts
- Heavy thunder hammer .... +15 pts
- Lightning claw .... +3 pts
- Meltagun .... +5 pts
- Missile launcher .... +15 pts
- Plasma gun .... +5 pts
- Plasma pistol .... +5 pts
- Power axe .... +3 pts
- Power fist .... +8 pts
- Power maul .... +3 pts
- Power sword .... +3 pts
- Stalker-pattern boltgun .... +3 pts
- Storm bolter .... +3 pts
- Storm shield .... +5 pts
- Thunder hammer .... +12 pts
- Xenophase blade .... +10 pts

Kill Team Cassius
Unit size .... 9 models
Unit cost .... 260 pts

ELITES

Deathwatch Terminator Squad
Unit size .... 5-10 models
Unit cost .... 33 pts/model
- Assault cannon .... +15 pts
- Chainfist .... +5 pts
- Cyclone missile launcher .... +20 pts
- Heavy flamer .... +10 pts
- Plasma cannon .... +15 pts
- Power fist .... +5 pts
- Deathwatch teleport homer .... +5 pts
- Thunder hammer .... +10 pts

FAST ATTACK

Veteran Bike Squad
Unit size .... 3-7 models
Unit cost .... 30 pts/model
- Deathwatch boltgun .... +5 pts
- Deathwatch combi-flamer .... +10 pts
- Deathwatch combi-grav .... +15 pts
- Deathwatch combi-melta .... +15 pts
- Deathwatch combi-plasma .... +15 pts
- Deathwatch shotgun .... +5 pts
- Flamer .... +5 pts
- Grav-gun .... +10 pts
- Grav-pistol .... +5 pts
- Inferno-pistol .... +5 pts
- Hand flamer .... +5 pts
- Heavy bolter .... +20 pts
- Lightning claw .... +5 pts
- Meltagun .... +10 pts
- Multi-melta .... +30 pts
- Plasma gun .... +10 pts
- Plasma pistol .... +5 pts
- Power axe .... +3 pts
- Power fist .... +10 pts
- Power maul .... +3 pts
- Power sword .... +3 pts
- Stalker-pattern boltgun .... +5 pts
- Storm bolter .... +5 pts
- Storm shield .... +5 pts
- Thunder hammer .... +15 pts
- Xenophase blade .... +10 pts

FLYER

Corvus Blackstar
Unit size .... 1 model
Unit cost .... 180 pts
- Auspex array .... +5 pts
- Hurricane bolter .... +15 pts
- Infernum halo-launcher .... +10 pts

Kill Team Specialisms
AQUILA	+15 pts
DOMINATUS	+20 pts
FUROR	+30 pts
MALLEUS	+30 pts
PURGATUS	+20 pts
VENATOR	+20 pts

GREY KNIGHTS

HQ

Brother-Captain
Unit size..1 model
Unit cost.......................................110 pts
- Incinerator..............................+5 pts
- Nemesis daemon hammer...........+10 pts
- Psilencer................................+5 pts
- Psycannon..............................+10 pts

Brother-Captain Stern
Unit size..1 model
Unit cost.......................................120 pts

Brotherhood Champion
Unit size..1 model
Unit cost...70 pts

Brotherhood Librarian
Unit size..1 model
Unit cost.......................................105 pts
- Combi-flamer..........................+10 pts
- Combi-melta............................+10 pts
- Combi-plasma..........................+10 pts
- Nemesis daemon hammer...........+10 pts
- Storm bolter............................+5 pts

Brotherhood Techmarine
Unit size..1 model
Unit cost...80 pts

Castellan Crowe
Unit size..1 model
Unit cost...90 pts

Grand Master
Unit size..1 model
Unit cost.......................................135 pts
- Incinerator..............................+5 pts
- Nemesis daemon hammer...........+10 pts
- Psilencer................................+5 pts
- Psycannon..............................+10 pts

Grand Master in Nemesis Dreadknight
Unit size..1 model
Unit cost.......................................150 pts
- Dreadknight Teleporter..............+10 pts
- Gatling Psilencer......................+20 pts
- Heavy incinerator.....................+15 pts
- Heavy psycannon......................+20 pts
- Nemesis daemon greathammer......+10 pts
- Nemesis greatsword..................+15 pts

Grand Master Voldus
Unit size..1 model
Unit cost.......................................150 pts

Brotherhood Chaplain
Unit size..1 model
Unit cost.......................................110 pts

Kaldor Draigo
Unit size..1 model
Unit cost.......................................180 pts

TROOPS

Brotherhood Terminator Squad
Unit size...............................5-10 models
Unit cost............................42 pts/model
- Incinerator..............................+5 pts
- Nemesis daemon hammer...........+10 pts
- Psilencer................................+5 pts
- Psycannon..............................+10 pts

Strike Squad
Unit size...............................5-10 models
Unit cost............................22 pts/model
- Nemesis daemon hammer...........+10 pts
- Psycannon..............................+5 pts

ELITES

Brotherhood Apothecary
Unit size..1 model
Unit cost.......................................100 pts
- Nemesis daemon hammer...........+10 pts

Brotherhood Ancient
Unit size..1 model
Unit cost.......................................100 pts
- Nemesis falchion......................+5 pts

Dreadnought
Unit size..1 model
Unit cost.......................................130 pts
- Heavy flamer...........................+10 pts
- Multi-melta.............................+5 pts
- Twin lascannon........................+20 pts

Paladin Ancient
Unit size..1 model
Unit cost.......................................110 pts
- Incinerator..............................+5 pts
- Nemesis falchion......................+5 pts
- Psilencer................................+10 pts
- Psycannon..............................+10 pts

Paladin Squad
Unit size...............................3-10 models
Unit cost............................47 pts/model
- Incinerator..............................+5 pts
- Nemesis daemon hammer...........+10 pts
- Psilencer................................+5 pts
- Psycannon..............................+10 pts

Purifier Squad
Unit size...............................5-10 models
Unit cost............................23 pts/model
- Nemesis daemon hammer...........+10 pts
- Psycannon..............................+5 pts

Servitors
Unit size.......................................4 models
Unit cost...30 pts
- Heavy bolter...........................+5 pts
- Multi-melta.............................+10 pts
- Plasma cannon.........................+5 pts

Venerable Dreadnought
Unit size..1 model
Unit cost.......................................145 pts
- Heavy flamer...........................+10 pts
- Multi-melta.............................+5 pts
- Twin lascannon........................+20 pts

FAST ATTACK

Interceptor Squad
Unit size...............................5-10 models
Unit cost............................24 pts/model
- Nemesis daemon hammer...........+10 pts
- Psycannon..............................+5 pts

HEAVY SUPPORT

Land Raider
Unit size..1 model
Unit cost.......................................265 pts
- Hunter-killer missile.................+5 pts
- Multi-melta.............................+25 pts
- Storm bolter............................+5 pts

Land Raider Crusader
Unit size..1 model
Unit cost.......................................265 pts
- Hunter-killer missile.................+5 pts
- Multi-melta.............................+25 pts
- Storm bolter............................+5 pts

Land Raider Redeemer
Unit size..1 model
Unit cost.......................................265 pts
- Hunter-killer missile.................+5 pts
- Multi-melta.............................+25 pts
- Storm bolter............................+5 pts

Nemesis Dreadknight
Unit size..1 model
Unit cost.......................................120 pts
- Dreadknight Teleporter..............+10 pts
- Gatling Psilencer......................+20 pts
- Heavy incinerator.....................+15 pts
- Heavy psycannon......................+20 pts
- Nemesis daemon greathammer......+10 pts
- Nemesis greatsword..................+15 pts

Purgation Squad
Unit size...............................5-10 models
Unit cost............................22 pts/model
- Nemesis daemon hammer...........+10 pts
- Psycannon..............................+5 pts

DEDICATED TRANSPORTS

Razorback
Unit size	1 model
Unit cost	110 pts/model
• Hunter-killer missile	+5 pts
• Storm bolter	+5 pts
• Twin assault cannon	+15 pts
• Twin lascannon	+10 pts

Rhino
Unit size	1 model
Unit cost	80 pts/model
• Additional storm bolter	+5 pts
• Hunter-killer missile	+5 pts

FLYERS

Stormhawk Interceptor
Unit size	1 model
Unit cost	185 pts
• Heavy bolter	+5 pts
• Las-talon	+25 pts
• Typhoon missile launcher	+20 pts

Stormraven Gunship
Unit size	1 model
Unit cost	290 pts
• Hurricane bolter	+15 pts
• Twin assault cannon	+10 pts
• Twin lascannon	+10 pts
• Twin Multi-melta	+20 pts
• Typhoon missile launcher	+10 pts

Stormtalon Gunship
Unit size	1 model
Unit cost	165 pts
• Heavy bolter	+5 pts
• Lascannon	+10 pts
• Typhoon missile launcher	+20 pts

Wisdom of the Prognosticars
Visions of the Augurium
• Augury of Aggression	+20 pts
• Heroism's Favour	+15 pts
• A Noble Death	+20 pts
• Omen of Incursion	+30 pts
• Presaged Paralysis	+15 pts
• Foretelling of Locus	+30 pts

Gifts of the Prescient
• True Name Shard	+10 pts
• Temporal Bombs	+15 pts
• Servant of the Throne	+20 pts
• Deluminator of Majesty	+15 pts
• Gem of Inoktu	+15 pts
• Severance Bolt	+30 pts

ADEPTA SORORITAS

HQ

Canoness
Unit size	1 model
Unit cost	50 pts
• Brazier of holy fire	+5 pts
• Blessed blade	+10 pts
• Condemnor boltgun	+10 pts
• Inferno pistol	+5 pts
• Null rod	+10 pts
• Plasma pistol	+5 pts
• Power sword	+5 pts
• Rod of office	+5 pts

Celestine and Geminae Superia
Unit size	3 models
Unit cost	200 pts

Ephrael Stern and Kyganil of the Bloody Tears
Unit size	2 models
Unit cost	120 pts

Junith Eruita
Unit size	1 model
Unit cost	130 pts

Missionary
Unit size	1 model
Unit cost	40 pts
• Power maul	+5 pts

Morvenn Vahl
Unit size	1 model
Unit cost	265 pts

Palatine
Unit size	1 model
Unit cost	45 pts
• Plasma pistol	+5 pts

Triumph of Saint Katherine
Unit size	1 model
Unit cost	220 pts

TROOPS

Battle Sisters Squad
Unit size	5-20 models
Unit cost	11 pts/model
• Artificer-crafted storm bolter	+5 pts
• Combi-melta	+10 pts
• Combi-plasma	+10 pts
• Condemnor boltgun	+10 pts
• Heavy bolter	+10 pts
• Incensor cherub	+5 pts
• Inferno pistol	+5 pts
• Meltagun	+10 pts
• Ministorum combi-flamer	+10 pts
• Ministorum hand flamer	+5 pts
• Ministorum heavy flamer	+10 pts
• Ministorum flamer	+5 pts
• Multi-melta	+20 pts
• Plasma pistol	+5 pts
• Power maul	+5 pts
• Power sword	+5 pts
• Simulacrum imperialis	+5 pts

ELITES

Aestred Thurga and Agathae Dolan
Unit size	2 models
Unit cost	90 pts

Arco-flagellants
Unit size	3-10 models
Unit cost	13 pts/model
• Endurant implants	+5 pts

Celestian Squad
Unit size	5-10 models
Unit cost	13 pts/model
• Artificer-crafted storm bolter	+5 pts
• Combi-melta	+10 pts
• Combi-plasma	+10 pts
• Condemnor boltgun	+10 pts
• Heavy bolter	+10 pts
• Incensor cherub	+5 pts
• Inferno pistol	+5 pts
• Meltagun	+10 pts
• Ministorum combi-flamer	+10 pts
• Ministorum hand flamer	+5 pts
• Ministorum heavy flamer	+10 pts
• Ministorum flamer	+5 pts
• Multi-melta	+20 pts
• Plasma pistol	+5 pts
• Power maul	+5 pts
• Power sword	+5 pts
• Simulacrum imperialis	+5 pts

Celestian Sacresants
Unit size	5-10 models
Unit cost	14 pts/model
• Inferno pistol	+5 pts
• Ministorum hand flamer	+5 pts
• Plasma pistol	+5 pts
• Spear of the faithful	+5 pts

Crusaders

Unit size.. 2-6 models
Unit cost...11 pts/model

Death Cult Assassins

Unit size.. 2-6 models
Unit cost...13 pts/model

Dialogus

Unit size..1 model
Unit cost..50 pts

Dogmata

Unit size..1 model
Unit cost..65 pts

Hospitaller

Unit size..1 model
Unit cost..50 pts

Imagifier

Unit size..1 model
Unit cost..50 pts

Paragon Warsuits

Unit size... 3 models
Unit cost.......................................240 pts/model
- Multi-melta .... +10 pts

Preacher

Unit size..1 model
Unit cost..25 pts
- Zealot's vindictor................................+5 pts

Repentia Superior

Unit size..1 model
Unit cost..40 pts

Sisters Repentia

Unit size.. 4-10 models
Unit cost...14 pts/model

FAST ATTACK

Dominion Squad

Unit size.. 5-10 models
Unit cost...12 pts/model
- Artificer-crafted storm bolter................ +5 pts
- Combi-melta.. +10 pts
- Combi-plasma....................................... +10 pts
- Condemnor boltgun .... +10 pts
- Incensor cherub .... +5 pts
- Inferno pistol.. +5 pts
- Meltagun .... +10 pts
- Ministorum combi-flamer.................... +10 pts
- Ministorum hand flamer .... +5 pts
- Ministorum flamer................................ +5 pts
- Plasma pistol .... +5 pts
- Power maul .... +5 pts
- Power sword .... +5 pts
- Simulacrum imperialis .... +5 pts

Seraphim Squad

Unit size.. 5-10 models
Unit cost...14 pts/model
- Inferno pistol.. +5 pts
- Ministorum hand flamer .... +5 pts
- Plasma pistol .... +5 pts
- Power sword .... +5 pts

Zephyrim Squad

Unit size.. 5-10 models
Unit cost...17 pts/model
- Plasma pistol .... +5 pts
- Zephyrim pennant.................................. +5 pts

HEAVY SUPPORT

Castigator

Unit size..1 model
Unit cost.. 160 pts
- Castigator battle cannon........................ +5 pts
- Hunter-killer missile .... +5 pts
- Storm bolter... +5 pts

Exorcist

Unit size..1 model
Unit cost.. 150 pts
- Exorcist missile launcher .... +30 pts
- Hunter-killer missile .... +5 pts

Mortifiers

Unit size..1-4 models
Unit cost...60 pts/model
- Anchorite sarcophagus........................... +5 pts

Penitent Engines

Unit size..1-4 models
Unit cost...55 pts/model

Retributor Squad

Unit size.. 5-10 models
Unit cost...12 pts/model
- Armorium cherub .... +5 pts
- Combi-melta... +10 pts
- Combi-plasma....................................... +10 pts
- Condemnor boltgun .... +10 pts
- Heavy bolter.. +10 pts
- Inferno pistol.. +5 pts
- Ministorum combi-flamer.................... +10 pts
- Ministorum hand flamer .... +5 pts
- Ministorum heavy flamer .... +10 pts
- Multi-melta .... +20 pts
- Plasma pistol .... +5 pts
- Power maul .... +5 pts
- Power sword .... +5 pts

DEDICATED TRANSPORT

Immolator

Unit size..1 model
Unit cost.. 120 pts
- Hunter-killer missile .... +5 pts
- Immolation flamers.............................. +10 pts
- Twin multi-melta .... +30 pts

Sororitas Rhino

Unit size..1 model
Unit cost..80 pts
- Hunter-killer missile .... +5 pts

FORTIFICATION

Battle Sanctum

Unit size..1 model
Unit cost..80 pts

Blessing of the Faithful

Word of the Emperor......................... +40 pts
Rapturous Blows .... +25 pts
Blinding Radiance.............................. +30 pts
The Emperor's Grace.......................... +20 pts
Righteous Judgement .... +25 pts
Divine Deliverance............................. +15 pts

ADEPTUS CUSTODES

HQ

Captain-General Trajann Valoris
Unit size .... 1 model
Unit cost .... 190 pts

Shield-Captain
Unit size .... 1 model
Unit cost .... 100 pts
- Castellan axe .... +5 pts
- Misericordia .... +3 pts
- Sentinel blade .... +2 pts
- Storm shield .... +10 pts

Shield-Captain in Allarus Terminator Armour
Unit size .... 1 model
Unit cost .... 110 pts
- Castellan axe .... +5 pts
- Misericordia .... +3 pts

Shield-Captain on Dawneagle Jetbike
Unit size .... 1 model
Unit cost .... 175 pts
- Misericordia .... +3 pts

TROOPS

Custodian Guard
Unit size .... 3-10 models
Unit cost .... 45 pts/model
- Misericordia .... +3 pts
- Sentinel blade .... +2 pts
- Storm shield .... +5 pts

ELITES

Allarus Custodians
Unit size .... 3-10 models
Unit cost .... 70 pts/model
- Castellan axe .... +5 pts
- Misericordia .... +3 pts

Custodian Wardens
Unit size .... 3-10 models
Unit cost .... 50 pts/model
- Castellan axe .... +5 pts

Venerable Contemptor Dreadnought
Unit size .... 1 model
Unit cost .... 155 pts

Vexilus Praetor
Unit size .... 1 model
Unit cost .... 105 pts
- Guardian spear .... +5 pts
- Castellan axe .... +10 pts
- Misericordia .... +3 pts
- Storm shield .... +10 pts
- Vexilla magnifica .... +10 pts

Vexilus Praetor in Allarus Terminator Armour
Unit size .... 1 model
Unit cost .... 115 pts
- Misericordia .... +3 pts
- Vexilla magnifica .... +10 pts

FAST ATTACK

Vertus Praetors
Unit size .... 3-10 models
Unit cost .... 85 pts/model
- Misericordia .... +3 pts

HEAVY SUPPORT

Venerable Land Raider
Unit size .... 1 model
Unit cost .... 280 pts
- Hunter-killer missile .... +5 pts
- Storm bolter .... +3 pts

SISTERS OF SILENCE

ELITES

Prosecutors
Unit size .... 5-10 models
Unit cost .... 12 pts/models

Vigilators
Unit size .... 5-10 models
Unit cost .... 17 pts/models

Witchseekers
Unit size .... 5-10 models
Unit cost .... 18 pts/models

DEDICATED TRANSPORT

Null-Maiden Rhino
Unit size .... 1 model
Unit cost .... 75 pts
- Hunter-killer missile .... +5 pts

OFFICIO ASSASSINORUM

ELITES

Callidus Assassin
Unit size .... 1 model
Unit cost .... 100 pts

Culexus Assassin
Unit size .... 1 model
Unit cost .... 100 pts

Eversor Assassin
Unit size .... 1 model
Unit cost .... 100 pts

Vindicare Assassin
Unit size .... 1 model
Unit cost .... 100 pts

ASTRA MILITARUM

HQ

Colonel 'Iron Hand' Straken
Unit size	1 model
Unit cost	80 pts

Commissar Yarrick
Unit size	1 model
Unit cost	105 pts

Company Commander
Unit size	1 model
Unit cost	35 pts
• Bolt pistol	+2 pts
• Boltgun	+2 pts
• Plasma pistol	+5 pts
• Power fist	+10 pts
• Power sword	+5 pts

Gaunt's Ghosts
Unit size	6 models
Unit cost	135 pts

Knight Commander Pask
Unit size	1 model
Unit cost	200 pts
• Battle cannon	+5 pts
• Augur array	+5 pts
• Demolisher cannon	+5 pts
• Dozer blade	+5 pts
• Exterminator autocannon	+15 pts
• Heavy bolter	+15 pts
• Heavy flamer	+15 pts
• Heavy stubber	+5 pts
• Hunter-killer missile	+5 pts
• Lascannon	+20 pts
• Multi-melta	+25 pts
• Plasma cannon	+20 pts
• Punisher gatling cannon	+20 pts
• Storm bolter	+3 pts
• Track guards	+5 pts

Lord Castellan Creed
Unit size	1 model
Unit cost	60 pts

Lord Commissar
Unit size	1 model
Unit cost	35 pts
• Power sword	+5 pts
• Boltgun	+2 pts
• Plasma pistol	+5 pts
• Power fist	+10 pts

Primaris Psyker
Unit size	1 model
Unit cost	50 pts

Tank Commander
Unit size	1 model
Unit cost	175 pts
• Battle cannon	+5 pts
• Augur array	+5 pts
• Demolisher cannon	+5 pts
• Dozer blade	+5 pts
• Exterminator autocannon	+15 pts
• Heavy bolter	+15 pts
• Heavy flamer	+15 pts
• Heavy stubber	+5 pts
• Hunter-killer missile	+5 pts
• Lascannon	+20 pts
• Multi-melta	+25 pts
• Plasma cannon	+20 pts
• Punisher gatling cannon	+20 pts
• Storm bolter	+3 pts
• Track guards	+5 pts

Tempestor Prime
Unit size	1 model
Unit cost	40 pts
• Bolt pistol	+2 pts
• Plasma pistol	+5 pts
• Power fist	+10 pts
• Power sword	+5 pts
• Tempestus command rod	+5 pts

TROOPS

Conscripts
Unit size	20-30 models
Unit cost	5 pts/model

Infantry Squad
Unit size	10 models
Unit cost	55 pts
• Autocannon	+10 pts
• Bolt pistol	+2 pts
• Boltgun	+2 pts
• Flamer	+5 pts
• Grenade launcher	+5 pts
• Heavy bolter	+10 pts
• Lascannon	+15 pts
• Meltagun	+5 pts
• Missile launcher	+15 pts
• Mortar	+10 pts
• Plasma gun	+5 pts
• Plasma pistol	+5 pts
• Power sword	+5 pts
• Sniper rifle	+2 pts
• Vox-caster	+5 pts

Militarum Tempestus Scions
Unit size	5-10 models
Unit cost	9 pts/model
• Bolt pistol	+2 pts
• Flamer	+5 pts
• Grenade launcher	+5 pts
• Hot-shot volley gun	+5 pts
• Meltagun	+10 pts
• Plasma gun	+10 pts
• Power fist	+10 pts
• Power sword	+5 pts
• Vox-caster	+5 pts

ELITES

Astropath
Unit size	1 model
Unit cost	35 pts

Bullgryns
Unit size	3-9 models
Unit cost	35 pts/model

Colour Sergeant Kell
Unit size	1 model
Unit cost	45 pts

Command Squad
Unit size	4 models
Unit cost	25 pts
• Autocannon	+10 pts
• Flamer	+5 pts
• Grenade launcher	+5 pts
• Heavy bolter	+10 pts
• Heavy flamer	+10 pts
• Lascannon	+15 pts
• Medi-pack	+5 pts
• Meltagun	+10 pts
• Missile launcher	+15 pts
• Mortar	+10 pts
• Plasma gun	+10 pts
• Regimental standard	+5 pts
• Sniper rifle	+2 pts
• Vox-caster	+5 pts

Commissar
Unit size	1 model
Unit cost	25 pts
• Boltgun	+2 pts
• Plasma pistol	+5 pts
• Power fist	+10 pts
• Power sword	+5 pts

Crusaders
Unit size	2-10 models
Unit cost	16 pts/model

Master of Ordnance
Unit size	1 model
Unit cost	35 pts

Militarum Tempestus Command Squad

Unit size	4 models
Unit cost	40 pts
• Flamer	+5 pts
• Grenade launcher	+5 pts
• Hot-shot volley gun	+5 pts
• Medi-pack	+5 pts
• Meltagun	+10 pts
• Plasma gun	+10 pts
• Platoon standard	+5 pts
• Vox-caster	+5 pts

Ministorum Priest

Unit size	1 model
Unit cost	40 pts

Nork Deddog

Unit size	1 model
Unit cost	60 pts

Officer of the Fleet

Unit size	1 model
Unit cost	25 pts

Ogryn Bodyguard

Unit size	1 model
Unit cost	50 pts
• Bullgryn maul	+5 pts
• Bullgryn plate	+5 pts
• Grenadier gauntlet	+5 pts

Ogryns

Unit size	3-9 models
Unit cost	25 pts/model

Platoon Commander

Unit size	1 model
Unit cost	25 pts
• Bolt pistol	+2 pts
• Boltgun	+2 pts
• Plasma pistol	+5 pts
• Power fist	+10 pts
• Power sword	+5 pts

Ratlings

Unit size	5-10 models
Unit cost	10 pts/model

Sergeant Harker

Unit size	1 model
Unit cost	55 pts

Servitors

Unit size	4 models
Unit cost	30 pts
• Heavy bolter	+5 pts
• Multi-melta	+15 pts
• Plasma cannon	+10 pts

Severina Raine

Unit size	1 model
Unit cost	35 pts

Sly Marbo

Unit size	1 model
Unit cost	60 pts

Special Weapons Squad

Unit size	6 models
Unit cost	40 pts
• Flamer	+3 pts
• Grenade launcher	+3 pts
• Meltagun	+3 pts
• Plasma gun	+3 pts

Tech-Priest Enginseer

Unit size	1 model
Unit cost	35 pts

Veterans

Unit size	10 models
Unit cost	65 pts
• Autocannon	+10 pts
• Bolt pistol	+2 pts
• Boltgun	+2 pts
• Flamer	+5 pts
• Grenade launcher	+5 pts
• Heavy bolter	+10 pts
• Heavy flamer	+10 pts
• Lascannon	+15 pts
• Meltagun	+10 pts
• Missile launcher	+15 pts
• Mortar	+10 pts
• Plasma gun	+10 pts
• Plasma pistol	+5 pts
• Power fist	+10 pts
• Power sword	+5 pts
• Sniper rifle	+2 pts
• Vox-caster	+5 pts

Wyrdvane Psykers

Unit size	3-9 models
Unit cost	8 pts/model

FAST ATTACK

Armoured Sentinels

Unit size	1-3 models
Unit cost	35 pts/model
• Autocannon	+10 pts
• Heavy flamer	+10 pts
• Hunter-killer missile	+5 pts
• Lascannon	+15 pts
• Missile launcher	+15 pts
• Plasma cannon	+15 pts
• Sentinel chainsaw	+2 pts

Hellhounds

Unit size	1-3 models
Unit cost (Bane Wolf)	100 pts/model
Unit cost (Devil Dog)	110 pts/model
Unit cost (Hellhound)	110 pts/model
• Augur array	+5 pts
• Dozer blade	+5 pts
• Heavy stubber	+5 pts
• Hunter-killer missile	+5 pts
• Multi-melta	+10 pts
• Storm bolter	+3 pts
• Track guards	+5 pts

Scout Sentinels

Unit size	1-3 models
Unit cost	35 pts/model
• Autocannon	+10 pts
• Heavy flamer	+10 pts
• Hunter-killer missile	+5 pts
• Lascannon	+15 pts
• Missile launcher	+15 pts
• Sentinel chainsaw	+2 pts

HEAVY SUPPORT

Basilisks

Unit size	1-3 models
Unit cost	125 pts/model
• Augur array	+5 pts
• Dozer blade	+5 pts
• Heavy stubber	+5 pts
• Hunter-killer missile	+5 pts
• Storm bolter	+3 pts
• Track guards	+5 pts

Deathstrike

Unit size	1 model
Unit cost	150 pts
• Augur array	+5 pts
• Dozer blade	+5 pts
• Heavy stubber	+5 pts
• Hunter-killer missile	+5 pts
• Storm bolter	+3 pts
• Track guards	+5 pts

Heavy Weapons Squad

Unit size	3 models
Unit cost	50 pts
• Lascannon	+5 pts
• Missile launcher	+5 pts

Hydras

Unit size	1-3 models
Unit cost	110 pts/model
• Augur array	+5 pts
• Dozer blade	+5 pts
• Heavy stubber	+5 pts
• Hunter-killer missile	+5 pts
• Storm bolter	+3 pts
• Track guards	+5 pts

Leman Russ Battle Tanks

Unit size	1-3 models
Unit cost	140 pts/model
• Augur array	+5 pts
• Battle cannon	+5 pts
• Demolisher cannon	+5 pts
• Dozer blade	+5 pts
• Exterminator autocannon	+15 pts
• Heavy bolter	+15 pts
• Heavy flamer	+15 pts
• Heavy stubber	+5 pts
• Hunter-killer missile	+5 pts
• Lascannon	+20 pts
• Multi-melta	+25 pts
• Plasma cannon	+20 pts
• Punisher gatling cannon	+20 pts
• Storm bolter	+3 pts
• Track guards	+5 pts

Manticore

Unit size .... 1 model

Unit cost .... 145 pts
- Augur array .... +5 pts
- Dozer blade .... +5 pts
- Heavy stubber .... +5 pts
- Hunter-killer missile .... +5 pts
- Storm bolter .... +3 pts
- Track guards .... +5 pts

Wyverns

Unit size .... 1-3 models

Unit cost .... 135 pts/model
- Augur array .... +5 pts
- Dozer blade .... +5 pts
- Heavy stubber .... +5 pts
- Hunter-killer missile .... +5 pts
- Storm bolter .... +3 pts
- Track guards .... +5 pts

DEDICATED TRANSPORT

Chimera

Unit size .... 1 model

Unit cost .... 65 pts
- Augur array .... +5 pts
- Dozer blade .... +5 pts
- Heavy bolter .... +10 pts
- Heavy flamer .... +10 pts
- Heavy stubber .... +5 pts
- Hunter-killer missile .... +5 pts
- Storm bolter .... +3 pts
- Track guards .... +5 pts

Taurox

Unit size .... 1 model

Unit cost .... 90 pts
- Heavy stubber .... +5 pts
- Storm bolter .... +3 pts

Taurox Prime

Unit size .... 1 model

Unit cost .... 115 pts
- Autocannon .... +5 pts
- Heavy stubber .... +5 pts
- Storm bolter .... +3 pts
- Taurox gatling cannon .... +5 pts
- Taurox missile launcher .... +15 pts

FLYERS

Valkyries

Unit size .... 1-3 models

Unit cost .... 120 pts/model
- Heavy bolter .... +15 pts
- Lascannon .... +15 pts

LORDS OF WAR

Baneblade

Unit size .... 1 model

Unit cost .... 410 pts
- Heavy stubber .... +5 pts
- Hunter-killer missile .... +5 pts
- Storm bolter .... +3 pts
- Lascannon .... +50 pts

Banehammer

Unit size .... 1 model

Unit cost .... 370 pts
- Heavy stubber .... +5 pts
- Hunter-killer missile .... +5 pts
- Storm bolter .... +3 pts
- Lascannon .... +50 pts

Banesword

Unit size .... 1 model

Unit cost .... 370 pts
- Heavy stubber .... +5 pts
- Hunter-killer missile .... +5 pts
- Storm bolter .... +3 pts
- Lascannon .... +50 pts

Doomhammer

Unit size .... 1 model

Unit cost .... 380 pts
- Heavy stubber .... +5 pts
- Hunter-killer missile .... +5 pts
- Storm bolter .... +3 pts
- Lascannon .... +50 pts

Hellhammer

Unit size .... 1 model

Unit cost .... 450 pts
- Heavy stubber .... +5 pts
- Hunter-killer missile .... +5 pts
- Storm bolter .... +3 pts
- Lascannon .... +50 pts

Shadowsword

Unit size .... 1 model

Unit cost .... 430 pts
- Heavy stubber .... +5 pts
- Hunter-killer missile .... +5 pts
- Storm bolter .... +3 pts
- Lascannon .... +50 pts

Stormlord

Unit size .... 1 model

Unit cost .... 430 pts
- Heavy stubber .... +5 pts
- Hunter-killer missile .... +5 pts
- Storm bolter .... +3 pts
- Lascannon .... +50 pts

Stormsword

Unit size .... 1 model

Unit cost .... 400 pts
- Heavy stubber .... +5 pts
- Hunter-killer missile .... +5 pts
- Storm bolter .... +3 pts
- Lascannon .... +50 pts

ADEPTUS MECHANICUS

HQ

Belisarius Cawl
Unit size..1 model
Unit cost.. 180 pts

Skitarii Marshal
Unit size..1 model
Unit cost.. 45 pts

Tech-Priest Dominus
Unit size..1 model
Unit cost.. 75 pts
• Eradication ray ....+5 pts
• Phosphor serpenta ....+5 pts

Tech-Priest Enginseer
Unit size..1 model
Unit cost.. 55 pts

Tech-Priest Manipulus
Unit size..1 model
Unit cost.. 70 pts
• Transonic cannon ....+5 pts

Technoarcheologist
Unit size..1 model
Unit cost.. 55 pts

TROOPS

Kataphron Breachers
Unit size...................................... 3-6 models
Unit cost..35 pts/model
• Torsion cannon .... +10 pts

Kataphron Destroyers
Unit size...................................... 3-6 models
Unit cost..40 pts/model
• Cognis flamer ....+5 pts
• Kataphron plasma culverin................ +10 pts

Skitarii Rangers
Unit size....................................5-20 models
Unit cost.. 8 pts/model
• Arc maul ....+5 pts
• Arc pistol ....+5 pts
• Arc rifle .... +10 pts
• Enhanced data-tether ....+5 pts
• Omnispex......................................+5 pts
• Phosphor blast pistol......................+5 pts
• Plasma caliver .... +10 pts
• Power sword ....+5 pts
• Taser goad ....+5 pts
• Transuranic arquebus...................... +15 pts

Skitarii Vanguard
Unit size....................................5-20 models
Unit cost.. 8 pts/model
• Arc maul ....+5 pts
• Arc pistol ....+5 pts
• Arc rifle .... +10 pts
• Enhanced data-tether ....+5 pts
• Omnispex......................................+5 pts
• Phosphor blast pistol......................+5 pts
• Plasma caliver .... +10 pts
• Power sword ....+5 pts
• Taser goad ....+5 pts
• Transuranic arquebus...................... +15 pts

ELITES

Corpuscarii Electro-Priests
Unit size....................................5-20 models
Unit cost.. 15 pts/model

Cybernetica Datasmith
Unit size..1 model
Unit cost.. 40 pts

Fulgurite Electro-Priests
Unit size....................................5-20 models
Unit cost.. 15 pts/model

Servitors
Unit size... 4 models
Unit cost.. 28 pts
• Heavy bolter................................. +10 pts
• Multi-melta.................................. +20 pts
• Plasma cannon.............................. +15 pts

Sicarian Infiltrators
Unit size.................................... 5-10 models
Unit cost.. 17 pts/model

Sicarian Ruststalkers
Unit size.................................... 5-10 models
Unit cost.. 17 pts/model

FAST ATTACK

Ironstrider Ballistarii
Unit size......................................1-6 models
Unit cost.. 65 pts/model
• Twin cognis lascannon.................... +10 pts

Pteraxii Skystalkers
Unit size.................................... 5-10 models
Unit cost.. 17 pts/model

Pteraxii Sterylizors
Unit size.................................... 5-10 models
Unit cost.. 19 pts/model

Serberys Raiders
Unit size...................................... 3-9 models
Unit cost.. 16 pts/model
• Enhanced data-tether ....+5 pts

Serberys Sulphurhounds
Unit size...................................... 3-9 models
Unit cost..20 pts/model
• Arc maul ....+5 pts
• Phosphor blast carbine.................. +10 pts
• Phosphor blast pistol......................+5 pts

Sydonian Dragoons
Unit size......................................1-6 models
Unit cost..55 pts/model
• Phosphor serpenta ....+5 pts
• Taser lance .... +15 pts

HEAVY SUPPORT

Kastelan Robots
Unit size...................................... 2-6 models
Unit cost.. 100 pts/model
• Kastelan phosphor blaster ....+5 pts

Onager Dunecrawler
Unit size..1 model
Unit cost.. 115 pts
• Cognis heavy stubber......................+5 pts

Skorpius Disintegrator
Unit size..1 model
Unit cost.. 145 pts

DEDICATED TRANSPORTS

Skorpius Dunerider
Unit size..1 model
Unit cost.. 95 pts

FLYERS

Archaeopter Fusilave
Unit size..1 model
Unit cost.. 130 pts
• Chaff launcher .... +20 pts

Archaeopter Stratoraptor
Unit size..1 model
Unit cost.. 160 pts
• Chaff launcher .... +20 pts

Archaeopter Transvector
Unit size..1 model
Unit cost.. 110 pts
• Chaff launcher .... +20 pts

Holy Orders
Genetors ....+25 pts
Logi..+35 pts
Magi...+30 pts
Artisans...+25 pts

IMPERIAL KNIGHTS

LORDS OF WAR

Armiger Helverin
Unit size...1-3 models
Unit cost.......................................155 pts/model
- Meltagun..+5 pts

Armiger Warglaive
Unit size...1-3 models
Unit cost.......................................135 pts/model
- Meltagun..+5 pts

Canis Rex
Unit size..1 model
Unit cost..430 pts

Knight Castellan
Unit size..1 model
Unit cost..605 pts
- Twin siegebreaker cannon ....+15 pts

Knight Crusader
Unit size..1 model
Unit cost..475 pts
- Ironstorm missile pod ....+15 pts
- Meltagun..+5 pts
- Rapid-fire battle cannon.....................+30 pts
- Stormspear rocket pod.......................+45 pts
- Twin Icarus autocannon.......................+30 pts

Knight Errant
Unit size..1 model
Unit cost..420 pts
- Ironstorm missile pod ....+15 pts
- Meltagun..+5 pts
- Stormspear rocket pod.........................+45 pts
- Thunderstrike gauntlet........................+5 pts
- Twin Icarus autocannon.......................+30 pts

Knight Gallant
Unit size..1 model
Unit cost..400 pts
- Ironstorm missile pod ....+15 pts
- Meltagun..+5 pts
- Stormspear rocket pod.......................+45 pts
- Twin Icarus autocannon.......................+30 pts

Knight Paladin
Unit size..1 model
Unit cost..450 pts
- Ironstorm missile pod ....+15 pts
- Meltagun..+5 pts
- Stormspear rocket pod.......................+45 pts
- Thunderstrike gauntlet........................+5 pts
- Twin Icarus autocannon.......................+30 pts

Knight Preceptor
Unit size..1 model
Unit cost..405 pts
- Ironstorm missile pod ....+15 pts
- Meltagun..+5 pts
- Stormspear rocket pod.......................+45 pts
- Thunderstrike gauntlet........................+5 pts
- Twin Icarus autocannon.......................+30 pts

Knight Valiant
Unit size..1 model
Unit cost..595 pts
- Twin siegebreaker cannon ....+15 pts

Knight Warden
Unit size..1 model
Unit cost..430 pts
- Ironstorm missile pod ....+15 pts
- Meltagun..+5 pts
- Stormspear rocket pod.......................+45 pts
- Thunderstrike gauntlet........................+5 pts
- Twin Icarus autocannon.......................+30 pts

FORTIFICATION

Sacristan Forgeshrine
Unit size..1 model
Unit cost..85 pts

INQUISITION

HQ

Inquisitor
Unit size..1 model
Unit cost..60 pts
- Combi-flamer ....+10 pts
- Combi-melta ....+10 pts
- Combi-plasma ....+10 pts
- Condemnor boltgun ....+10 pts
- Flamer..+5 pts
- Force axe ....+10 pts
- Force stave ....+10 pts
- Force sword ....+10 pts
- Incinerator ....+10 pts
- Inferno pistol ....+5 pts
- Meltagun...+10 pts
- Nemesis Daemon hammer ....+20 pts
- Plasma gun..+10 pts
- Plasma pistol ....+5 pts
- Power fist ....+10 pts
- Power maul ....+5 pts
- Power sword ....+5 pts
- Storm bolter...+5 pts
- Thunder hammer ....+15 pts

Inquisitor Coteaz
Unit size..1 model
Unit cost..95 pts

Inquisitor Eisenhorn
Unit size..1 model
Unit cost..85 pts

Inquisitor Greyfax
Unit size..1 model
Unit cost..90 pts

Inquisitor Karamazov
Unit size..1 model
Unit cost..125 pts

Lord Inquisitor Kyria Draxus
Unit size..1 model
Unit cost..85 pts

Ordo Malleus Inquisitor in Terminator Armour
Unit size..1 model
Unit cost..95 pts
- Combi-flamer ....+10 pts
- Combi-melta ....+10 pts
- Combi-plasma ....+10 pts
- Force axe ....+10 pts
- Force stave ....+10 pts
- Force sword ....+10 pts
- Nemesis Daemon hammer ....+20 pts
- Psycannon...+10 pts
- Storm bolter...+5 pts

ELITES

Acolytes
Unit size...1-6 models
Unit cost.......................................10 pts/model
- Combi-flamer ....+10 pts
- Combi-melta ....+10 pts
- Combi-plasma ....+10 pts
- Flamer..+5 pts
- Meltagun...+10 pts
- Plasma gun..+10 pts
- Plasma pistol ....+5 pts
- Power fist ....+10 pts
- Power maul ....+5 pts
- Power sword ....+5 pts
- Storm bolter...+5 pts
- Thunder hammer ....+15 pts

Daemonhost
Unit size..1 model
Unit cost..25 pts

Jokaero Weaponsmith
Unit size..1 model
Unit cost..20 pts

CHAOS SPACE MARINES

HQ

Abaddon the Despoiler
Unit size...1 model
Unit cost.. 220 pts

Chaos Lord
Unit size...1 model
Unit cost.. 80 pts
- Chainaxe..+1 pt
- Combi-bolter....................................+3 pts
- Combi-flamer..................................+10 pts
- Combi-melta....................................+10 pts
- Combi-plasma..................................+10 pts
- Jump pack.......................................+25 pts
- Lightning claw..................................+5 pts
- Plasma pistol....................................+5 pts
- Power axe...+5 pts
- Power fist.......................................+10 pts
- Power maul.......................................+5 pts
- Power sword......................................+5 pts
- Thunder hammer..............................+20 pts

Chaos Lord in Terminator Armour
Unit size...1 model
Unit cost.. 100 pts
- Chainfist..+5 pts
- Combi-flamer....................................+5 pts
- Combi-melta......................................+5 pts
- Combi-plasma....................................+5 pts
- Power fist..+5 pts

Cypher
Unit size...1 model
Unit cost.. 85 pts

Daemon Prince
Unit size...1 model
Unit cost.. 150 pts
- Daemonic axe...................................+10 pts
- Hellforged sword..............................+10 pts
- Malefic talons (one set/two sets) +0/+15 pts
- Warp bolter.......................................+5 pts
- Wings..+35 pts

Dark Apostle
Unit size...1 model
Unit cost.. 80 pts

Exalted Champion
Unit size...1 model
Unit cost.. 75 pts
- Chainaxe..+1 pt
- Combi-bolter....................................+3 pts
- Combi-flamer..................................+10 pts
- Combi-melta....................................+10 pts
- Combi-plasma..................................+10 pts
- Lightning claw..................................+5 pts
- Plasma pistol....................................+5 pts
- Power axe...+5 pts
- Power fist.......................................+10 pts
- Power maul.......................................+5 pts
- Power sword......................................+5 pts
- Thunder hammer..............................+20 pts

Fabius Bile
Unit size...1 model
Unit cost.. 90 pts

This unit can also include:
Surgeon Acolyte.....................................+5 pts

Haarken Worldclaimer
Unit size...1 model
Unit cost.. 95 pts

Huron Blackheart
Unit size...1 model
Unit cost.. 110 pts

Khârn the Betrayer
Unit size...1 model
Unit cost.. 115 pts

Lord Discordant on Helstalker
Unit size...1 model
Unit cost.. 195 pts
- Baleflamer...+5 pts
- Magma cutter....................................+5 pts

Lucius the Eternal
Unit size...1 model
Unit cost.. 95 pts

Master of Executions
Unit size...1 model
Unit cost.. 65 pts

Master of Possession
Unit size...1 model
Unit cost.. 95 pts

Sorcerer
Unit size...1 model
Unit cost.. 90 pts
- Chainaxe..+1 pt
- Combi-bolter....................................+3 pts
- Combi-flamer..................................+10 pts
- Combi-melta....................................+10 pts
- Combi-plasma..................................+10 pts
- Jump pack.......................................+25 pts
- Lightning claw..................................+5 pts
- Plasma pistol....................................+5 pts
- Power axe...+5 pts
- Power fist.......................................+10 pts
- Power maul.......................................+5 pts
- Power sword......................................+5 pts
- Thunder hammer..............................+20 pts

Sorcerer in Terminator Armour
Unit size...1 model
Unit cost.. 105 pts
- Chainfist..+5 pts
- Combi-flamer....................................+5 pts
- Combi-melta......................................+5 pts
- Combi-plasma....................................+5 pts
- Power fist..+5 pts

Warpsmith
Unit size...1 model
Unit cost.. +65 pts
- Combi-bolter....................................+3 pts
- Combi-flamer..................................+10 pts
- Combi-melta....................................+10 pts
- Combi-plasma..................................+10 pts
- Plasma pistol....................................+5 pts
- Power axe...+5 pts

TROOPS

Chaos Cultists
Unit size................................... 10-30 models
Unit cost...................................... 5 pts/model
- Flamer...+5 pts
- Heavy stubber...................................+5 pts

Chaos Space Marines
Unit size..................................... 5-20 models
Unit cost..14 pts/model
- Autocannon.....................................+10 pts
- Chainaxe..+1 pt
- Combi-bolter....................................+3 pts
- Combi-flamer..................................+10 pts
- Combi-melta....................................+10 pts
- Combi-plasma..................................+10 pts
- Flamer...+5 pts
- Heavy bolter....................................+10 pts
- Icon of Despair.................................+10 pts
- Icon of Excess..................................+10 pts
- Icon of Flame....................................+5 pts
- Icon of Vengeance.............................+5 pts
- Icon of Wrath....................................+10 pts
- Lascannon..+15 pts
- Lightning claw..................................+5 pts
- Meltagun...+10 pts
- Missile launcher...............................+15 pts
- Plasma gun......................................+10 pts
- Plasma pistol....................................+5 pts
- Power axe...+5 pts
- Power fist.......................................+10 pts
- Power maul.......................................+5 pts
- Power sword......................................+5 pts
- Reaper chaincannon.........................+20 pts

ELITES

Chosen
Unit size .... 5-10 models
Unit cost .... 14 pts/model
- Autocannon .... +10 pts
- Chainaxe .... +1 pt
- Combi-bolter .... +3 pts
- Combi-flamer .... +10 pts
- Combi-melta .... +10 pts
- Combi-plasma .... +10 pts
- Flamer .... +5 pts
- Heavy bolter .... +10 pts
- Icon of Despair .... +10 pts
- Icon of Excess .... +10 pts
- Icon of Flame .... +5 pts
- Icon of Vengeance .... +5 pts
- Icon of Wrath .... +10 pts
- Lascannon .... +15 pts
- Lightning claw .... +3 pts
- Meltagun .... +10 pts
- Missile launcher .... +15 pts
- Plasma gun .... +10 pts
- Plasma pistol .... +5 pts
- Power axe .... +3 pts
- Power fist .... +10 pts
- Power maul .... +3 pts
- Power sword .... +3 pts
- Reaper chaincannon .... +20 pts
- Thunder hammer .... +12 pts

Dark Disciples
Unit size .... 2 models
Unit cost .... 5 pts/model

Fallen
Unit size .... 5-10 models
Unit cost .... 14 pts/model
- Autocannon .... +10 pts
- Chainaxe .... +1 pt
- Combi-bolter .... +3 pts
- Combi-flamer .... +10 pts
- Combi-melta .... +10 pts
- Combi-plasma .... +10 pts
- Flamer .... +5 pts
- Heavy bolter .... +10 pts
- Lascannon .... +15 pts
- Lightning claw .... +5 pts
- Meltagun .... +10 pts
- Missile launcher .... +15 pts
- Plasma gun .... +10 pts
- Plasma pistol .... +5 pts
- Power axe .... +3 pts
- Power fist .... +8 pts
- Power maul .... +3 pts
- Power sword .... +3 pts
- Thunder hammer .... +12 pts

Greater Possessed
Unit size .... 1-2 models
Unit cost .... 65 pts/model

Helbrute
Unit size .... 1 model
Unit cost .... 110 pts
- Combi-bolter .... +5 pts
- Heavy flamer .... +10 pts
- Multi-melta .... +5 pts
- Twin heavy bolter .... +10 pts
- Twin lascannon .... +20 pts

Khorne Berzerkers
Unit size .... 5-20 models
Unit cost .... 17 pts/model
- Chainaxe .... +1 pt
- Combi-bolter .... +3 pts
- Combi-flamer .... +10 pts
- Combi-melta .... +10 pts
- Combi-plasma .... +10 pts
- Icon of Wrath .... +10 pts
- Lightning claw .... +5 pts
- Plasma pistol .... +5 pts
- Power axe .... +5 pts
- Power fist .... +10 pts
- Power maul .... +5 pts
- Power sword .... +5 pts

Mutilators
Unit size .... 3 models
Unit cost .... 35 pts/model

Noise Marines
Unit size .... 5-20 models
Unit cost .... 16 pts/model
- Blastmaster .... +10 pts
- Chainaxe .... +1 pt
- Combi-bolter .... +3 pts
- Combi-flamer .... +10 pts
- Combi-melta .... +10 pts
- Combi-plasma .... +10 pts
- Doom siren .... +10 pts
- Icon of Excess .... +10 pts
- Lightning claw .... +5 pts
- Plasma pistol .... +5 pts
- Power axe .... +5 pts
- Power fist .... +10 pts
- Power maul .... +5 pts
- Power sword .... +5 pts
- Sonic blaster .... +5 pts

Plague Marines
Unit size .... 5-20 models
Unit cost .... 18 pts/model
- Blight launcher .... +10 pts
- Bubotic axe .... +5 pts
- Flail of corruption .... +15 pts
- Great plague cleaver .... +15 pts
- Icon of Despair .... +10 pts
- Mace of contagion .... +5 pts
- Meltagun .... +10 pts
- Plague belcher .... +5 pts
- Plague spewer .... +10 pts
- Plasma gun .... +10 pts
- Plasma pistol .... +5 pts
- Power fist .... +10 pts

Possessed
Unit size .... 5-20 models
Unit cost .... 20 pts/model
- Icon of Despair .... +10 pts
- Icon of Excess .... +10 pts
- Icon of Flame .... +5 pts
- Icon of Vengeance .... +5 pts
- Icon of Wrath .... +10 pts

Rubric Marines
Unit size .... 5-20 models
Unit cost .... 18 pts/model
- Icon of Flame .... +5 pts
- Plasma pistol .... +5 pts
- Soulreaper cannon .... +10 pts
- Warpflame pistol .... +5 pts
- Warpflamer .... +8 pts

Terminators
Unit size .... 5-10 models
Unit cost .... 28 pts/model
- Chainfist .... +5 pts
- Combi-flamer .... +5 pts
- Combi-melta .... +5 pts
- Combi-plasma .... +5 pts
- Heavy flamer .... +5 pts
- Icon of Despair .... +10 pts
- Icon of Excess .... +10 pts
- Icon of Flame .... +5 pts
- Icon of Vengeance .... +5 pts
- Icon of Wrath .... +10 pts
- Power fist .... +5 pts
- Reaper autocannon .... +5 pts

FAST ATTACK

Bikers
Unit size .... 3-9 models
Unit cost .... 25 pts/model
- Chainaxe .... +1 pt
- Combi-bolter .... +3 pts
- Combi-flamer .... +10 pts
- Combi-melta .... +10 pts
- Combi-plasma .... +10 pts
- Flamer .... +5 pts
- Icon of Despair .... +10 pts
- Icon of Excess .... +10 pts
- Icon of Flame .... +5 pts
- Icon of Vengeance .... +5 pts
- Icon of Wrath .... +10 pts
- Lightning claw .... +5 pts
- Meltagun .... +10 pts
- Plasma gun .... +10 pts
- Plasma pistol .... +5 pts
- Power axe .... +5 pts
- Power fist .... +10 pts
- Power maul .... +5 pts
- Power sword .... +5 pts

Chaos Spawn
Unit size .... 1-5 models
Unit cost .... 23 pts/model

Raptors
Unit size...5-15 models
Unit cost..15 pts/model
- Chainaxe ....+1 pt
- Combi-bolter..+3 pts
- Combi-flamer.....................................+10 pts
- Combi-melta.......................................+10 pts
- Combi-plasma.....................................+10 pts
- Flamer..+5 pts
- Icon of Despair...................................+10 pts
- Icon of Excess....................................+10 pts
- Icon of Flame......................................+5 pts
- Icon of Vengeance...............................+5 pts
- Icon of Wrath......................................+10 pts
- Lightning claw.....................................+5 pts
- Meltagun...+10 pts
- Plasma gun...+10 pts
- Plasma pistol.......................................+5 pts
- Power axe...+5 pts
- Power fist..+10 pts
- Power maul..+5 pts
- Power sword...+5 pts

Warp Talons
Unit size...5-10 models
Unit cost..23 pts/model

HEAVY SUPPORT

Chaos Land Raider
Unit size...1 model
Unit cost.. 265 pts
- Combi-bolter..+3 pts
- Combi-flamer.....................................+10 pts
- Combi-melta.......................................+10 pts
- Combi-plasma.....................................+10 pts
- Havoc launcher....................................+5 pts

Chaos Predator
Unit size...1 model
Unit cost.. 130 pts
- Combi-bolter..+3 pts
- Combi-flamer.....................................+10 pts
- Combi-melta.......................................+10 pts
- Combi-plasma.....................................+10 pts
- Havoc launcher....................................+5 pts
- Heavy bolter......................................+15 pts
- Lascannon...+20 pts
- Twin lascannon...................................+10 pts

Chaos Vindicator
Unit size...1 model
Unit cost.. 130 pts
- Combi-bolter..+3 pts
- Combi-flamer.....................................+10 pts
- Combi-melta.......................................+10 pts
- Combi-plasma.....................................+10 pts
- Havoc launcher....................................+5 pts

Defiler
Unit size...1 model
Unit cost.. 135 pts
- Combi-bolter..+3 pts
- Combi-flamer.....................................+10 pts
- Combi-melta.......................................+10 pts
- Combi-plasma.....................................+10 pts
- Defiler scourge....................................+5 pts
- Twin heavy bolter...............................+20 pts
- Twin heavy flamer...............................+25 pts
- Twin lascannon...................................+30 pts

Forgefiend
Unit size...1 model
Unit cost.. 85 pts
- Ectoplasma cannon.............................+20 pts
- Hades autocannon...............................+25 pts

Havocs
Unit size...5 models
Unit cost.. 85 pts
- Autocannon..+10 pts
- Chainaxe ....+1 pt
- Combi-bolter..+3 pts
- Combi-flamer.....................................+10 pts
- Combi-melta.......................................+10 pts
- Combi-plasma.....................................+10 pts
- Flamer..+5 pts
- Heavy bolter......................................+10 pts
- Lascannon...+15 pts
- Lightning claw.....................................+5 pts
- Meltagun...+10 pts
- Missile launcher..................................+15 pts
- Plasma gun...+10 pts
- Plasma pistol.......................................+5 pts
- Power axe...+5 pts
- Power fist..+10 pts
- Power maul..+5 pts
- Power sword...+5 pts
- Reaper chaincannon ....+20 pts

Maulerfiend
Unit size...1 model
Unit cost.. 140 pts

Obliterators
Unit size...1-3 models
Unit cost..105 pts/model

Venomcrawler
Unit size...1 model
Unit cost.. 110 pts

DEDICATED TRANSPORT

Chaos Rhino
Unit size...1 model
Unit cost.. 80 pts
- Combi-flamer.....................................+10 pts
- Combi-melta.......................................+10 pts
- Combi-plasma.....................................+10 pts
- Extra combi-bolter................................+5 pts
- Havoc launcher....................................+5 pts

FLYERS

Heldrake
Unit size...1 model
Unit cost.. 150 pts
- Hades autocannon.................................+5 pts

LORDS OF WAR

Khorne Lord of Skulls
Unit size...1 model
Unit cost.. 435 pts
- Daemongore cannon.............................+15 pts
- Gorestorm cannon.................................+5 pts
- Hades gatling cannon...........................+30 pts

FORTIFICATION

Noctilith Crown
Unit size...1 model
Unit cost.. 85 pts

DAEMONS

Bloodletters
Unit size...10-30 models
Unit cost..8 pts/model
- Daemonic Icon...................................+15 pts
- Instrument of Chaos ....+10 pts

Daemonettes
Unit size...10-30 models
Unit cost..7 pts/model
- Daemonic Icon...................................+15 pts
- Instrument of Chaos ....+10 pts

Horrors
Unit size...10-30 models
Unit cost (Blue Horrors) ....7 pts/model
Unit cost (Iridescent Horror).......................8 pts
Unit cost (Pair of Brimstone Horrors) 5 pts/model
Unit cost (Pink Horrors)....................8 pts/model
- Daemonic Icon...................................+15 pts
- Instrument of Chaos ....+10 pts

Plaguebearers
Unit size...10-30 models
Unit cost..9 pts/model
- Daemonic Icon...................................+15 pts
- Instrument of Chaos ....+10 pts

DEATH GUARD

HQ

Death Guard Chaos Lord
Unit size .... 1 model
Unit cost .... 85 pts
- Balesword .... +10 pts
- Combi-flamer .... +10 pts
- Combi-melta .... +10 pts
- Combi-plasma .... +10 pts
- Lightning claw .... +5 pts
- Power axe .... +5 pts
- Power fist .... +10 pts
- Power maul .... +5 pts
- Power sword .... +5 pts

Death Guard Chaos Lord in Terminator Armour
Unit size .... 1 model
Unit cost .... 105 pts
- Chainfist .... +10 pts
- Combi-melta .... +5 pts
- Power fist .... +5 pts

Death Guard Daemon Prince
Unit size .... 1 model
Unit cost .... 140 pts
- Daemonic axe .... +10 pts
- Hellforged sword .... +10 pts
- Plague spewer .... +5 pts
- Foetid wings .... +35 pts

Death Guard Sorcerer in Terminator Armour
Unit size .... 1 model
Unit cost .... 110 pts
- Chainfist .... +15 pts
- Combi-melta .... +5 pts
- Power fist .... +10 pts

Lord of Contagion
Unit size .... 1 model
Unit cost .... 120 pts
- Orb of desiccation .... +5 pts

Lord of Virulence
Unit size .... 1 model
Unit cost .... 120 pts

Malignant Plaguecaster
- Unit size .... 1 model
- Unit cost .... 95 pts

Typhus
- Unit size .... 1 model
- Unit cost .... 165 pts

TROOPS

Death Guard Cultists
Unit size .... 10-30 models
Unit cost .... 5 pts/model
- Flamer .... +5 pts
- Heavy stubber .... +5 pts

Plague Marines
Unit size .... 5-10 models
Unit cost .... 21 pts/model
- Blight launcher .... +10 pts
- Bubotic axe .... +3 pts
- Flail of corruption .... +10 pts
- Great plague cleaver .... +10 pts
- Icon of despair .... +10 pts
- Mace of contagion .... +5 pts
- Meltagun .... +10 pts
- Plague belcher .... +5 pts
- Plague spewer .... +10 pts
- Plasma gun .... +10 pts
- Plasma pistol .... +5 pts
- Power fist .... +10 pts
- Sigil of decay .... +10 pts

Poxwalkers
Unit size .... 10-20 models
Unit cost .... 5 pts/model

ELITES

Biologus Putrifier
Unit size .... 1 model
Unit cost .... 65 pts

Blightlord Terminators
Unit size .... 5-10 models
Unit cost .... 40 pts/model
- Blight launcher .... +5 pts
- Combi-flamer .... +5 pts
- Combi-melta .... +5 pts
- Combi-plasma .... +5 pts
- Flail of corruption .... +5 pts
- Plague spewer .... +5 pts
- Reaper autocannon .... +5 pts

Death Guard Possessed
Unit size .... 5-10 models
Unit cost .... 24 pts/model

Deathshroud Terminators
Unit size .... 3-6 models
Unit cost .... 50 pts/model
- Additional plaguespurt gauntlet .... +5 pts
- Chimes of contagion .... +15 pts

Foul Blightspawn
Unit size .... 1 model
Unit cost .... 75 pts

Helbrute
Unit size .... 1 model
Unit cost .... 115 pts
- Combi-bolter .... +5 pts
- Heavy flamer .... +10 pts
- Multi-melta .... +5 pts
- Twin heavy bolter .... +10 pts
- Twin lascannon .... +20 pts

Noxious Blightbringer
Unit size .... 1 model
Unit cost .... 60 pts

Plague Surgeon
Unit size .... 1 model
Unit cost .... 75 pts

Tallyman
Unit size .... 1 model
Unit cost .... 70 pts

FAST ATTACK

Chaos Spawn
Unit size .... 1-5 models
Unit cost .... 23 pts/model

Foetid Bloat-drone
Unit size .... 1 model
Unit cost .... 130 pts
- Fleshmower .... +5 pts
- Heavy blight launcher .... +10 pts

Myphitic Blight-haulers
Unit size .... 1-3 models
Unit cost .... 140 pts/model

HEAVY SUPPORT

Chaos Land Raider
Unit size .... 1 model
Unit cost .... 265 pts
- Combi-bolter .... +5 pts
- Combi-flamer .... +10 pts
- Combi-melta .... +10 pts
- Combi-plasma .... +10 pts
- Havoc launcher .... +5 pts

Chaos Predator Annihilator
Unit size .... 1 model
Unit cost .... 130 pts
- Combi-bolter .... +5 pts
- Combi-flamer .... +10 pts
- Combi-melta .... +10 pts
- Combi-plasma .... +10 pts
- Havoc launcher .... +5 pts
- Heavy bolter .... +15 pts
- Lascannon .... +20 pts

Chaos Predator Destructor

Unit size	1 model
Unit cost	140 pts
• Combi-bolter	+5 pts
• Combi-flamer	+10 pts
• Combi-melta	+10 pts
• Combi-plasma	+10 pts
• Havoc launcher	+5 pts
• Heavy bolter	+15 pts
• Lascannon	+20 pts

Defiler

Unit size	1 model
Unit cost	165 pts
• Combi-bolter	+5 pts
• Combi-flamer	+10 pts
• Combi-melta	+10 pts
• Combi-plasma	+10 pts
• Defiler scourge	+10 pts
• Twin heavy bolter	+10 pts
• Twin heavy flamer	+15 pts
• Twin lascannon	+20 pts

Plagueburst Crawler

Unit size	1 model
Unit cost	165 pts
• Entropy cannon	+5 pts

DEDICATED TRANSPORTS

Chaos Rhino

Unit size	1 model
Unit cost	80 pts
• Additional combi-bolter	+5 pts
• Combi-flamer	+10 pts
• Combi-melta	+10 pts
• Combi-plasma	+10 pts
• Havoc launcher	+5 pts

LORDS OF WAR

Mortarion

Unit size	1 model
Unit cost	490 pts

FORTIFICATIONS

Miasmic Malignifier

Unit size	1 model
Unit cost	75 pts

Deadly Pathogens

Acidic Malady	+20 pts
Explosive Outbreak	+20 pts
Virulent Fever	+20 pts
Befouling Runoff	+10 pts
Unstable Sickness	+15 pts
Corrosive Filth	+20 pts
Viscous Death	+10 pts

THOUSAND SONS

HQ

Ahriman

Unit size	1 model
Unit cost	160 pts
• Disc of Tzeentch	+20 pts

Exalted Sorcerer

Unit size	1 model
Unit cost	100 pts
• Disc of Tzeentch	+25 pts
• Plasma pistol	+5 pts
• Prosperine khopesh	+5 pts
• Warpflame pistol	+5 pts

Infernal Master

Unit size	1 model
Unit cost	90 pts

Sorcerer

Unit size	1 model
Unit cost	90 pts
• Plasma pistol	+5 pts
• Warpflame pistol	+5 pts

Sorcerer in Terminator Armour

Unit size	1 model
Unit cost	105 pts
• Inferno combi-melta	+5 pts

Thousand Sons Daemon Prince

Unit size	1 model
Unit cost	140 pts
• Daemonic Axe	+10 pts
• Hellforged Sword	+10 pts
• Wings	+35 pts

TROOPS

Rubric Marines

Unit size	5-10 models
Unit cost	21 pts/model
• Icon of flame	+10 pts
• Plasma pistol	+5 pts
• Soulreaper cannon	+10 pts
• Warpflame pistol	+5 pts
• Warpflamer	+6 pts

Thousand Sons Cultists

Unit size	10-30 models
Unit cost	5 pts/model
• Flamer	+5 pts
• Heavy stubber	+5 pts

Tzaangors

Unit size	10-20 models
Unit cost	7 pts/model
• Brayhorn	+10 pts
• Herd banner	+5 pts

ELITES

Helbrute

Unit size	1 model
Unit cost	115 pts
• Heavy flamer	+10 pts
• Inferno combi-bolter	+5 pts
• Multi-melta	+5 pts
• Twin heavy bolter	+10 pts
• Twin lascannon	+20 pts

Scarab Occult Terminators

Unit size	5-10 models
Unit cost	40 pts/model
• Heavy warpflamer	+5 pts
• Hellfyre missile rack	+10 pts
• Soulreaper cannon	+5 pts

Tzaangor Shaman

Unit size	1 model
Unit cost	70 pts

FAST ATTACK

Chaos Spawn
Unit size .... 1-5 models
Unit cost .... 23 pts/model

Tzaangor Enlightened
Unit size .... 3-6 models
Unit cost .... 18 pts/model

HEAVY SUPPORT

Chaos Land Raider
Unit size .... 1 model
Unit cost .... 265 pts
- Havoc launcher .... +5 pts
- Inferno combi-bolter .... +5 pts
- Inferno combi-flamer .... +10 pts
- Inferno combi-melta .... +10 pts

Chaos Predator Annihilator
Unit size .... 1 model
Unit cost .... 130 pts
- Havoc launcher .... +5 pts
- Heavy bolter .... +15 pts
- Inferno combi-bolter .... +5 pts
- Inferno combi-flamer .... +10 pts
- Inferno combi-melta .... +10 pts
- Lascannon .... +20 pts

Chaos Predator Destructor
Unit size .... 1 model
Unit cost .... 140 pts
- Havoc launcher .... +5 pts
- Heavy bolter .... +15 pts
- Inferno combi-bolter .... +5 pts
- Inferno combi-flamer .... +10 pts
- Inferno combi-melta .... +10 pts
- Lascannon .... +20 pts

Chaos Vindicator
Unit size .... 1 model
Unit cost .... 130 pts
- Havoc launcher .... +5 pts
- Inferno combi-bolter .... +5 pts
- Inferno combi-flamer .... +10 pts
- Inferno combi-melta .... +10 pts
- Vindicator siege shield .... +10 pts

Defiler
Unit size .... 1 model
Unit cost .... 165 pts
- Defiler scourge .... +10 pts
- Inferno combi-bolter .... +5 pts
- Inferno combi-flamer .... +10 pts
- Inferno combi-melta .... +10 pts
- Twin heavy bolter .... +10 pts
- Twin heavy flamer .... +15 pts
- Twin lascannon .... +20 pts

Forgefiend
Unit size .... 1 model
Unit cost .... 110 pts
- Ectoplasma cannon .... +15 pts
- Heavy hades autocannon .... +25 pts

Maulerfiend
Unit size .... 1 model
Unit cost .... 140 pts
- Lasher Tendrils .... +10 pts

Mutalith Vortex Beast
Unit size .... 1 model
Unit cost .... 145 pts

DEDICATED TRANSPORT

Chaos Rhino
Unit size .... 1 model
Unit cost .... 80 pts
- Additional inferno combi-bolter .... +5 pts
- Havoc launcher .... +5 pts
- Inferno combi-flamer .... +10 pts
- Inferno combi-melta .... +10 pts

FLYERS

Heldrake
Unit size .... 1 model
Unit cost .... 165 pts

LORD OF WAR

Magnus the Red
Unit size .... 1 model
Unit cost .... 450 pts

Legion Command
Ardent Automata .... +20 pts
Battle-psyker .... +10 pts
Dilettante .... +35 pts
Loyal Thrall .... +15 pts
Paradigm of Change .... +15 pts
Protégé .... +10 pts
Rehati .... +25 pts
Rites of Coalescence .... +15 pts
Witch-warrior .... +15 pts

CHAOS DAEMONS

HQ

Be'lakor
Unit size....................................1 model
Unit cost.................................. 360 pts

Bloodmaster
Unit size....................................1 model
Unit cost....................................60 pts

Bloodthirster of Insensate Rage
Unit size....................................1 model
Unit cost.................................. 250 pts

Bloodthirster of Unfettered Fury
Unit size....................................1 model
Unit cost.................................. 240 pts

Blood Throne
Unit size....................................1 model
Unit cost.................................. 115 pts

The Blue Scribes
Unit size....................................1 model
Unit cost....................................90 pts

Changecaster
Unit size....................................1 model
Unit cost....................................85 pts
• Staff of change.......................+5 pts

The Changeling
Unit size....................................1 model
Unit cost.................................. 105 pts

Contorted Epitome
Unit size....................................1 model
Unit cost.................................. 210 pts

Daemon Prince
Unit size....................................1 model
Unit cost.................................. 150 pts
• Daemonic axe.......................+10 pts
• Malefic talons (one set/two sets) +0/+15 pts
• Wings..................................+35 pts

Epidemius
Unit size....................................1 model
Unit cost.................................. 105 pts

Fateskimmer
Unit size....................................1 model
Unit cost.................................. 160 pts
• Chanting horrors....................+5 pts
• Staff of change.......................+5 pts

Fluxmaster
Unit size....................................1 model
Unit cost.................................. 105 pts
• Staff of change.......................+5 pts

Great Unclean One
Unit size....................................1 model
Unit cost.................................. 240 pts
• Bilesword............................+10 pts
• Bileblade............................+10 pts
• Doomsday bell......................+20 pts
• Plague flail.........................+20 pts

Herald of Slaanesh
Unit size....................................1 model
Unit cost....................................55 pts

Herald of Slaanesh on Exalted Seeker Chariot
Unit size....................................1 model
Unit cost.................................. 130 pts

Herald of Slaanesh on Hellflayer
Unit size....................................1 model
Unit cost.................................. 105 pts

Herald of Slaanesh on Seeker Chariot
Unit size....................................1 model
Unit cost....................................95 pts

Horticulous Slimux
Unit size....................................1 model
Unit cost.................................. 160 pts

Infernal Enrapturess
Unit size....................................1 model
Unit cost....................................75 pts

Kairos Fateweaver
Unit size....................................1 model
Unit cost.................................. 270 pts

Karanak
Unit size....................................1 model
Unit cost....................................75 pts

Keeper of Secrets
Unit size....................................1 model
Unit cost.................................. 230 pts
• Shining aegis.......................+10 pts

Lord of Change
Unit size....................................1 model
Unit cost.................................. 290 pts
• Baleful sword.........................+5 pts
• Rod of sorcery......................+10 pts

The Masque of Slaanesh
Unit size....................................1 model
Unit cost....................................85 pts

Poxbringer
Unit size....................................1 model
Unit cost....................................75 pts

Rotigus
Unit size....................................1 model
Unit cost.................................. 270 pts

Shalaxi Helbane
Unit size....................................1 model
Unit cost.................................. 240 pts
• Shining aegis.......................+10 pts

Skarbrand
Unit size....................................1 model
Unit cost.................................. 310 pts

Skullmaster
Unit size....................................1 model
Unit cost....................................95 pts

Skulltaker
Unit size....................................1 model
Unit cost....................................90 pts

Sloppity Bilepiper
Unit size....................................1 model
Unit cost....................................65 pts

Spoilpox Scrivener
Unit size....................................1 model
Unit cost.................................. 100 pts

Syll'Esske, the Vengeful Allegiance
Unit size....................................1 model
Unit cost.................................. 230 pts

Wrath of Khorne Bloodthirster
Unit size....................................1 model
Unit cost.................................. 230 pts

TROOPS

Bloodletters
Unit size...........................10-30 models
Unit cost........................... 8 pts/model
• Daemonic Icon......................+15 pts
• Instrument of Chaos...............+10 pts

Daemonettes
Unit size...........................10-30 models
Unit cost........................... 7 pts/model
• Daemonic Icon......................+15 pts
• Instrument of Chaos...............+10 pts

Horrors
Unit size...........................10-30 models
Unit cost (Blue Horrors)........ 7 pts/model
Unit cost (Iridescent Horror).............8 pts
Unit cost (Pair of Brimstone Horrors) 5 pts/model
Unit cost (Pink Horrors)........ 8 pts/model
• Daemonic Icon......................+15 pts
• Instrument of Chaos...............+10 pts

Nurglings
Unit size.............................3-9 models
Unit cost...........................22 pts/model

Plaguebearers

Unit size .... 10-30 models
Unit cost .... 9 pts/model
- Daemonic Icon .... +15 pts
- Instrument of Chaos .... +10 pts

ELITES

Beasts of Nurgle

Unit size .... 1-9 models
Unit cost .... 35 pts/model

Bloodcrushers

Unit size .... 3-12 models
Unit cost .... 40 pts/model
- Daemonic Icon .... +15 pts
- Instrument of Chaos .... +10 pts

Exalted Flamer

Unit size .... 1 model
Unit cost .... 60 pts

Fiends

Unit size .... 1-9 models
Unit cost (Fiends) .... 40 pts/model
Unit cost (Blissbringer) .... 45 pts/model

Flamers

Unit size .... 3-9 models
Unit cost .... 23 pts/model

FAST ATTACK

Chaos Spawn*

Unit size .... 1 model
Unit cost .... 23 pts

Furies

Unit size .... 5-20 models
Unit cost .... 9 pts/model

Flesh Hounds

Unit size .... 5-20 models
Unit cost (Flesh Hounds) .... 18 pts/model
Unit cost (Gore Hound) .... 28 pts/model

Hellflayer

Unit size .... 1 model
Unit cost .... 80 pts

Plague Drones

Unit size .... 3-9 models
Unit cost .... 35 pts/model
- Daemonic Icon .... +15 pts
- Instrument of Chaos .... +10 pts

Screamers

Unit size .... 3-9 models
Unit cost .... 26 pts/model

Seekers

Unit size .... 5-20 models
Unit cost .... 18 pts/model
- Daemonic Icon .... +15 pts
- Instrument of Chaos .... +10 pts

Designer's Note: *This points value is only
included in case a rule transforms a model into
a Chaos Spawn and its points value is required
for any rules purpose.*

HEAVY SUPPORT

Burning Chariot

Unit size .... 1 model
Unit cost .... 110 pts
- Chanting Horrors .... +5 pts

Exalted Seeker Chariot

Unit size .... 1 model
Unit cost .... 80 pts

Seeker Chariot

Unit size .... 1 model
Unit cost .... 60 pts

Skull Cannon

Unit size .... 1 model
Unit cost .... 90 pts

Soul Grinder

Unit size .... 1 model
Unit cost .... 175 pts

FORTIFICATION

Feculent Gnarlmaws

Unit size .... 1-3 models
Unit cost .... 95 pts/model

Skull Altar

Unit size .... 1 model
Unit cost .... 110 pts

CHAOS KNIGHTS

LORDS OF WAR

Knight Desecrator

Unit size .... 1 model
Unit cost .... 405 pts
- Thunderstrike gauntlet .... +5 pts

Knight Despoiler

Unit size .... 1 model
Unit cost .... 310 pts
- Avenger gatling cannon
  (single/pair) .... +90 /+200 pts
- Heavy stubber .... +5 pts
- Ironstorm missile pod .... +15 pts
- Meltagun .... +10 pts
- Rapid-fire battle cannon .... +100 pts
- Reaper chainsword .... +30 pts
- Stormspear rocket pod .... +45 pts
- Thermal cannon .... +75 pts
- Thunderstrike gauntlet .... +35 pts
- Twin Icarus autocannon .... +30 pts

Knight Despoiler with 1 reaper chainsword and 1 thunderstrike gauntlet

Unit size .... 1 model
Unit cost .... 400 pts
- Ironstorm missile pod .... +15 pts
- Meltagun .... +5 pts
- Stormspear rocket pod .... +45 pts
- Twin Icarus autocannon .... +30 pts

Knight Rampager

Unit size .... 1 model
Unit cost .... 415 pts

Knight Tyrant

Unit size .... 1 model
Unit cost .... 595 pts
- Twin siegebreaker cannon .... +15 pts
- Volcano lance .... +10 pts

War Dog

Unit size .... 1-3 models
Unit cost .... 135 pts/model
- Meltagun .... +5 pts
- War Dog autocannon .... +10 pts

CRAFTWORLDS

HQ

Asurmen
Unit size .... 1 model
Unit cost .... 160 pts

Autarch
Unit size .... 1 model
Unit cost .... 80 pts

Autarch Skyrunner
Unit size .... 1 model
Unit cost .... 105 pts
- Fusion gun .... +10 pts
- Laser lance .... +5 pts

Autarch with Swooping Hawk Wings
Unit size .... 1 model
Unit cost .... 90 pts

Avatar of Khaine
Unit size .... 1 model
Unit cost .... 200 pts

Baharroth
Unit size .... 1 model
Unit cost .... 120 pts

Eldrad Ulthran
Unit size .... 1 model
Unit cost .... 155 pts

Farseer
Unit size .... 1 model
Unit cost .... 115 pts
- Singing spear .... +5 pts

Farseer Skyrunner
Unit size .... 1 model
Unit cost .... 135 pts
- Singing spear .... +5 pts

Fuegan
Unit size .... 1 model
Unit cost .... 135 pts

Illic Nightspear
Unit size .... 1 model
Unit cost .... 70 pts

Jain Zar
Unit size .... 1 model
Unit cost .... 125 pts

Karandras
Unit size .... 1 model
Unit cost .... 135 pts

Maugan Ra
Unit size .... 1 model
Unit cost .... 150 pts

Prince Yriel
Unit size .... 1 model
Unit cost .... 85 pts

Spiritseer
Unit size .... 1 model
Unit cost .... 60 pts

Warlock
Unit size .... 1 model
Unit cost .... 50 pts
- Singing spear .... +5 pts

Warlock Conclave
Unit size .... 2-10 models
Unit cost .... 40 pts/model
- Singing spear .... +5 pts

Warlock Skyrunner
Unit size .... 1 model
Unit cost .... 65 pts
- Singing spear .... +5 pts

Warlock Skyrunner Conclave
Unit size .... 2-10 models
Unit cost .... 55 pts/model
- Singing spear .... +5 pts

TROOPS

Dire Avengers
Unit size .... 5-10 models
Unit cost .... 11 pts/model
- Shimmershield .... +5 pts

Guardian Defenders
Unit size (Guardian) .... 10-20 models
Unit cost (Guardian) .... 8 pts/model
Unit size (Heavy Weapon Platform) .... 0-2 models
Unit cost (Heavy Weapon Platform) ...... 12 pts/model
- Aeldari missile launcher .... +20 pts
- Bright lance .... +20 pts
- Scatter laser .... +10 pts
- Shuriken cannon .... +10 pts
- Starcannon .... +15 pts

Rangers
Unit size .... 5-10 models
Unit cost .... 13 pts/model

Storm Guardians
Unit size .... 8-24 models
Unit cost .... 7 pts/model
- Flamer .... +5 pts
- Fusion gun .... +10 pts

ELITES

Fire Dragons
Unit size .... 5-10 models
Unit cost .... 20 pts/model
- Dragon's breath flamer .... +10 pts
- Firepike .... +15 pts

Howling Banshees
Unit size .... 5-10 models
Unit cost .... 15 pts/model
- Executioner .... +5 pts
- Triskele .... +5 pts

Striking Scorpions
Unit size .... 5-10 models
Unit cost .... 13 pts/model
- Biting blade .... +5 pts
- Scorpion's claw .... +10 pts

Wraithblades
Unit size .... 5-10 models
Unit cost .... 37 pts/model

Wraithguard
Unit size .... 5-10 models
Unit cost .... 35 pts/model
- D-scythe .... +10 pts

FAST ATTACK

Shining Spears
Unit size .... 3-9 models
Unit cost .... 35 pts/model
- Star lance .... +5 pts

Swooping Hawks
Unit size .... 5-10 models
Unit cost .... 16 pts/model
- Hawk's talon .... +5 pts
- Power sword .... +5 pts

Vypers
Unit size .... 1-3 models
Unit cost .... 40 pts/model
- Aeldari missile launcher .... +20 pts
- Bright lance .... +20 pts
- Scatter laser .... +10 pts
- Shuriken cannon .... +10 pts
- Starcannon .... +15 pts

Warp Spiders
Unit size .... 5-10 models
Unit cost .... 18 pts/model
- Powerblades .... +5 pts

Windriders
Unit size .... 3-9 models
Unit cost .... 20 pts/model
- Scatter laser .... +10 pts
- Shuriken cannon .... +10 pts

HEAVY SUPPORT

Dark Reapers
Unit size .... 3-10 models
Unit cost .... 32 pts/model
- Aeldari missile launcher .... +20 pts
- Tempest launcher .... +10 pts

Falcon
Unit size .... 1 model
Unit cost .... 115 pts
- Aeldari missile launcher .... +20 pts
- Bright lance .... +20 pts
- Crystal targeting matrix .... +5 pts
- Scatter laser .... +10 pts
- Shuriken cannon .... +10 pts
- Spirit stones .... +10 pts
- Star engines .... +10 pts
- Starcannon .... +15 pts
- Vectored engines .... +10 pts

Fire Prism
Unit size .... 1 model
Unit cost .... 155 pts
- Crystal targeting matrix .... +5 pts
- Shuriken cannon .... +10 pts
- Spirit stones .... +10 pts
- Star engines .... +10 pts
- Vectored engines .... +10 pts

Night Spinner
Unit size .... 1 model
Unit cost .... 135 pts
- Crystal targeting matrix .... +5 pts
- Shuriken cannon .... +10 pts
- Spirit stones .... +10 pts
- Star engines .... +10 pts
- Vectored engines .... +10 pts

Support Weapons (including crew)
Unit size .... 1-3 models
Unit cost .... 45 pts/model
- D-cannon .... +25 pts
- Shadow weaver .... +5 pts

War Walkers
Unit size .... 1-3 models
Unit cost .... 60 pts/model
- Aeldari missile launcher .... +10 pts
- Bright lance .... +10 pts
- Starcannon .... +5 pts

Wraithlord
Unit size .... 1 model
Unit cost .... 100 pts
- Aeldari missile launcher .... +20 pts
- Bright lance .... +20 pts
- Flamer .... +5 pts
- Ghostglaive .... +10 pts
- Scatter laser .... +10 pts
- Shuriken cannon .... +10 pts
- Starcannon .... +15 pts

DEDICATED TRANSPORT

Wave Serpent
Unit size .... 1 model
Unit cost .... 130 pts
- Crystal targeting matrix .... +5 pts
- Shuriken cannon .... +10 pts
- Spirit stones .... +10 pts
- Star engines .... +10 pts
- Twin Aeldari missile launcher .... +40 pts
- Twin bright lance .... +40 pts
- Twin scatter laser .... +20 pts
- Twin shuriken cannon .... +20 pts
- Twin starcannon .... +30 pts
- Vectored engines .... +10 pts

FLYERS

Crimson Hunter
Unit size .... 1 model
Unit cost .... 180 pts

Crimson Hunter Exarch
Unit size .... 1 model
Unit cost .... 170 pts
- Bright lance .... +20 pts
- Starcannon .... +15 pts

Hemlock Wraithfighter
Unit size .... 1 model
Unit cost .... 240 pts

LORDS OF WAR

Wraithknight
Unit size .... 1 model
Unit cost .... 315 pts
- Heavy wraithcannon .... +50 pts
- Scatter laser .... +10 pts
- Scattershield .... +15 pts
- Shuriken cannon .... +10 pts
- Starcannon .... +15 pts
- Suncannon .... +60 pts
- Titanic ghostglaive .... +30 pts

FORTIFICATION

Webway Gate
Unit size .... 1 model
Unit cost .... 95 pts

DRUKHARI

HQ

Archon
Unit size.................................1 model
Unit cost..65 pts
- Blast pistol.................................+5 pts
- Huskblade..................................+5 pts

Drazhar
Unit size.................................1 model
Unit cost......................................135 pts

Haemonculus
Unit size.................................1 model
Unit cost..80 pts

Lelith Hesperax
Unit size.................................1 model
Unit cost..90 pts

Succubus
Unit size.................................1 model
Unit cost..60 pts

Urien Rakarth
Unit size.................................1 model
Unit cost......................................100 pts

TROOPS

Kabalite Warriors
Unit size.....................................5-20
Unit cost................................8 pts/model
- Agoniser....................................+5 pts
- Blast pistol.................................+5 pts
- Blaster.....................................+10 pts
- Dark lance................................+15 pts
- Phantasm grenade launcher.................+5 pts
- Power sword................................+5 pts
- Shredder....................................+5 pts
- Splinter cannon...........................+10 pts

Wyches
Unit size.....................................5-20
Unit cost...............................10 pts/model
- Agoniser....................................+5 pts
- Blast pistol.................................+5 pts
- Hydra gauntlets.............................+5 pts
- Phantasm grenade launcher.................+5 pts
- Power sword................................+5 pts
- Razorflails.................................+5 pts
- Shardnet and impaler......................+10 pts

Wracks
- Unit size....................................5-20
- Unit cost..............................8 pts/model
- Agoniser....................................+5 pts
- Electrocorrosive whip.......................+5 pts
- Flesh gauntlet..............................+5 pts
- Hexrifle....................................+5 pts
- Liquifier gun..............................+10 pts
- Mindphase gauntlet..........................+5 pts
- Ossefactor..................................+5 pts
- Scissorhand................................+10 pts
- Stinger pistol..............................+5 pts
- Venom blade.................................+5 pts

Favoured Retinues
- Kabalite Trueborn............+2 pts/model
- Hekatrix Bloodbrides......+2 pts/model
- Haemoxytes..................+2 pts/model

ELITES

Beastmaster
Unit size.................................1 model
Unit cost..40 pts

Court of the Archon
Unit size.....................................4-16
Unit cost.......................................
- Lhamaean........................16 pts/model
- Medusae..........................22 pts/model
- Sslyth...........................18 pts/model
- Ur-Ghul..........................16 pts/model

Grotesques
Unit size......................................3-6
Unit cost...............................40 pts/model
- Liquifier gun................................+5 pts

Incubi
Unit size.....................................5-10
Unit cost..............................16 pts/model

Mandrakes
Unit size.....................................5-10
Unit cost..............................15 pts/model

FAST ATTACK

Clawed Fiends
Unit size......................................1-6
Unit cost..............................25 pts/model

Hellions
Unit size.....................................5-20
Unit cost..............................17 pts/model
- Agoniser....................................+5 pts
- Phantasm grenade launcher.................+5 pts
- Power sword................................+5 pts
- Stunclaw....................................+5 pts

Khymerae
Unit size......................................2-6
Unit cost..............................10 pts/model

Razorwing Flock
- Unit size....................................3-9
- Unit cost.............................12 pts/model

Reavers
Unit size.....................................3-12
Unit cost..............................20 pts/model
- Agoniser....................................+5 pts
- Blaster.....................................+10 pts
- Cluster caltrops............................+5 pts
- Grav-talon..................................+5 pts
- Heat lance.................................+10 pts
- Power sword................................+5 pts

Scourges
- Unit size...................................5-10
- Unit cost.............................12 pts/model
- Agoniser....................................+5 pts
- Blast pistol................................+5 pts
- Blaster.....................................+10 pts
- Dark lance.................................+15 pts
- Drukhari haywire blaster...................+10 pts
- Heat lance.................................+10 pts
- Shredder....................................+5 pts
- Splinter cannon...........................+10 pts
- Power lance.................................+5 pts
- Venom blade.................................+5 pts

HEAVY SUPPORT

Cronos
Unit size......................................1-3
Unit cost..............................70 pts/model
- Spirit probe................................+5 pts
- Spirit vortex..............................+10 pts

Ravager
Unit size.................................1 model
Unit cost......................................140 pts
- Chain-snares................................+5 pts
- Disintegrator cannon........................+5 pts
- Grisly trophies.............................+5 pts
- Phantasm grenade launcher.................+5 pts
- Shock prow..................................+5 pts

Talos
Unit size......................................1-3
Unit cost.............................110 pts/model
- Talos gauntlet..............................+5 pts
- Twin liquifier gun.........................+15 pts

DEDICATED TRANSPORTS

Raider
Unit size... 1 model
Unit cost..85 pts
- Chain-snares...................................+5 pts
- Disintegrator cannon ....+5 pts
- Grisly trophies ....+5 pts
- Phantasm grenade launcher................+5 pts
- Shock prow......................................+5 pts
- Splinter racks..............................+10 pts

Venom
Unit size... 1 model
Unit cost..65 pts
- Chain-snares...................................+5 pts
- Grisly trophies ....+5 pts
- Splinter cannon............................+10 pts

FLYERS

Razorwing Jetfighter
Unit size... 1 model
Unit cost..160 pts
- Disintegrator cannon ....+5 pts
- Splinter cannon.............................+5 pts

Voidraven Bomber
Unit size... 1 model
Unit cost..185 pts
- Dark scythe....................................+5 pts
- Voidraven missiles ....+15 pts

HARLEQUINS

HQ

Shadowseer
Unit size..1 model
Unit cost... 115 pts
- Neuro disruptor..............................+5 pts

Troupe Master
Unit size..1 model
Unit cost... 65 pts
- Fusion pistol...................................+5 pts
- Harlequin's caress..........................+6 pts
- Harlequin's embrace.......................+5 pts
- Harlequin's kiss..............................+6 pts
- Power sword ....+5 pts
- Neuro disruptor..............................+5 pts

TROOPS

Troupe
Unit size....................................... 5-12 models
Unit cost.................................14 pts/model
- Fusion pistol...................................+5 pts
- Harlequin's caress..........................+6 pts
- Harlequin's embrace.......................+5 pts
- Harlequin's kiss..............................+6 pts
- Neuro disruptor..............................+5 pts

ELITES

Death Jester
Unit size..1 model
Unit cost... 50 pts

Solitaire
Unit size..1 model
Unit cost... 100 pts

FAST ATTACK

Skyweavers
Unit size..................................... 2-6 models
Unit cost..................................45 pts/model
- Haywire cannon ....+5 pts
- Zephyrglaive ....+5 pts

HEAVY SUPPORT

Voidweaver
Unit size..1 model
Unit cost... 90 pts

DEDICATED TRANSPORT

Starweaver
Unit size..1 model
Unit cost... 80 pts

FORTIFICATION

Webway Gate
Unit size..1 model
Unit cost... 95 pts

YNNARI

HQ

The Visarch
Unit size..1 model
Unit cost... 85 pts

The Yncarne
Unit size..1 model
Unit cost... 290 pts

Yvraine
Unit size..1 model
Unit cost... 120 pts

NECRONS

HQ

Anrakyr the Traveller
Unit size .... 1 model
Unit cost .... 140 pts

Catacomb Command Barge
Unit size .... 1 model
Unit cost .... 155 pts
- Gauss cannon .... +5 pts
- Resurrection orb .... +30 pts
- Warscythe .... +5 pts

Chronomancer
Unit size .... 1 model
Unit cost .... 80 pts
- Entropic lance .... +10 pts

Illuminor Szeras
Unit size .... 1 model
Unit cost .... 160 pts

Imotekh the Stormlord
Unit size .... 1 model
Unit cost .... 145 pts

Lokhust Lord
Unit size .... 1 model
Unit cost .... 105 pts
- Phylactery .... +5 pts
- Resurrection orb .... +30 pts
- Warscythe .... +5 pts

Lord
Unit size .... 1 model
Unit cost .... 70 pts
- Resurrection orb .... +30 pts
- Warscythe .... +5 pts

Nemesor Zahndrekh
Unit size .... 1 model
Unit cost .... 135 pts

Orikan the Diviner
Unit size .... 1 model
Unit cost .... 110 pts

Overlord
Unit size .... 1 model
Unit cost .... 95 pts
- Resurrection orb .... +30 pts
- Tachyon arrow .... +5 pts
- Voidscythe .... +15 pts
- Warscythe .... +5 pts

Plasmancer
Unit size .... 1 model
Unit cost .... 70 pts

Psychomancer
Unit size .... 1 model
Unit cost .... 70 pts

Royal Warden
Unit size .... 1 model
Unit cost .... 75 pts

Skorpekh Lord
Unit size .... 1 model
Unit cost .... 130 pts

Technomancer
Unit size .... 1 model
Unit cost .... 75 pts
- Canoptek cloak .... +5 pts
- Canoptek control node .... +15 pts

Trazyn the Infinite
Unit size .... 1 model
Unit cost .... 100 pts

Vargard Obyron
Unit size .... 1 model
Unit cost .... 100 pts

Cryptek Arkana
Atavindicator .... +25 pts
Cortical subjugator scarabs .... +15 pts
Countertemporal nanomines .... +30 pts
Cryptogeometric adjuster .... +15 pts
Dimensional sanctum .... +15 pts
Fail-safe overcharger .... +30 pts
Hypermaterial ablator .... +25 pts
Metalodermal tesla weave .... +20 pts
Photonic transubjector .... +20 pts
Phylacterine hive .... +20 pts
Prismatic obfuscatron .... +20 pts
Quantum orb .... +20 pts

TROOPS

Immortals
Unit size .... 5-10 models
Unit cost .... 17 pts/model

Necron Warriors
Unit size .... 10-20 models
Unit cost .... 13 pts/model

ELITES

C'tan Shard of the Deceiver
Unit size .... 1 model
Unit cost .... 350 pts

C'tan Shard of the Nightbringer
Unit size .... 1 model
Unit cost .... 370 pts

C'tan Shard of the Void Dragon
Unit size .... 1 model
Unit cost .... 350 pts

Canoptek Plasmacyte
Unit size .... 1 model
Unit cost .... 15 pts

Canoptek Reanimator
Unit size .... 1 model
Unit cost .... 80 pts

Canoptek Spyders
Unit size .... 1-3 models
Unit cost .... 60 pts/model
- Fabricator claw array .... +5 pts
- Gloom prism .... +5 pts
- Particle beamer .... +5 pts

Cryptothralls
Unit size .... 2 models
Unit cost .... 40 pts

Deathmarks
Unit size .... 5-10 models
Unit cost .... 18 pts/model

Flayed Ones
Unit size .... 5-20 models
Unit cost .... 13 pts/model

Hexmark Destroyer
Unit size .... 1 model
Unit cost .... 75 pts

Lychguard
Unit size .... 5-10 models
Unit cost .... 28 pts/model

Skorpekh Destroyers
Unit size .... 3-6 models
Unit cost .... 35 pts/model

Transcendent C'tan
Unit size .... 1 model
Unit cost .... 270 pts

Triarch Stalker
Unit size .... 1 model
Unit cost .... 135 pts
- Heat ray .... +5 pts
- Twin heavy gauss cannon .... +15 pts

FAST ATTACK

Canoptek Scarab Swarms
Unit size..............................3-9 models
Unit cost..........................15 pts/model

Canoptek Wraiths
Unit size..............................3-6 models
Unit cost..........................35 pts/model
- Particle caster.............................+5 pts
- Transdimensional beamer.................+10 pts

Ophydian Destroyers
Unit size..............................3-6 models
Unit cost..........................35 pts/model

Tomb Blades
Unit size..............................3-9 models
Unit cost..........................25 pts/model
- Nebuloscope.............................+3 pts
- Shadowloom.............................+5 pts
- Shieldvanes.............................+3 pts
- Twin gauss blaster.............................+5 pts
- Twin tesla carbine.............................+5 pts

Triarch Praetorians
Unit size..............................5-10 models
Unit cost..........................25 pts/model

HEAVY SUPPORT

Annihilation Barge
Unit size..............................1 model
Unit cost..........................120 pts
- Gauss cannon.............................+5 pts

Canoptek Doomstalker
Unit size..............................1 model
Unit cost..........................140 pts

Doomsday Ark
Unit size..............................1 model
Unit cost..........................170 pts

Lokhust Destroyers
Unit size..............................1-7 models
Unit cost..........................50 pts/model
- Enmitic exterminator.............................+10 pts
- Gauss destructor.............................+10 pts

Lokhust Heavy Destroyers
Unit size..............................1-3 models
Unit cost..........................60 pts/model

DEDICATED TRANSPORTS

Ghost Ark
Unit size..............................1 model
Unit cost..........................145 pts

FLYERS

Doom Scythe
Unit size..............................1 model
Unit cost..........................200 pts

Night Scythe
Unit size..............................1 model
Unit cost..........................145 pts

LORDS OF WAR

Monolith
Unit size..............................1 model
Unit cost..........................360 pts
- Death ray.............................+5 pts

Obelisk
Unit size..............................1 model
Unit cost..........................370 pts

The Silent King
Unit size..............................3 models
Unit cost..........................450 pts

Tesseract Vault
Unit size..............................1 model
Unit cost..........................500 pts

FORTIFICATIONS

Convergence of Dominion
Unit size..............................3 models
Unit cost..........................120 pts

ORKS

HQ

Big Mek in Mega Armour
Unit size..............................1 model
Unit cost..........................85 pts
- Grot Oiler.............................+5 pts
- Killsaw.............................+10 pts
- Kombi-weapon with rokkit launcha...+10 pts
- Kombi-weapon with skorcha.............+15 pts
- Kustom force field.............................+20 pts
- Kustom mega-blasta.............................+10 pts
- Kustom shoota.............................+3 pts
- Power klaw.............................+10 pts
- Tellyport blasta.............................+10 pts

Big Mek with Shokk Attack Gun
Unit size..............................1 model
Unit cost..........................120 pts
- Grot Oiler.............................+5 pts

Big Mek with Kustom Force Field
Unit size..............................1 model
Unit cost..........................60 pts
- Grot Oiler.............................+5 pts

Boss Snikrot
Unit size..............................1 model
Unit cost..........................75 pts

Boss Zagstruk
Unit size..............................1 model
Unit cost..........................95 pts

Deffkilla Wartrike
Unit size..............................1 model
Unit cost..........................125 pts

Ghazghkull Thraka
Unit size..............................1 model
Unit cost..........................300 pts

Kaptin Badrukk
Unit size..............................1 model
Unit cost..........................90 pts
- Ammo Runt.............................+5 pts

Makari
Unit size..............................1 model
Unit cost..........................65 pts

Warboss
Unit size..............................1 model
Unit cost..........................70 pts
- Big choppa.............................+5 pts
- Kombi-weapon with rokkit launcha...+10 pts
- Kombi-weapon with skorcha.............+15 pts
- Kustom shoota.............................+3 pts
- Power klaw.............................+10 pts

Weirdboy
Unit size..............................1 model
Unit cost..........................75 pts

TROOPS

Boyz
Unit size .... 10-30 models
Unit cost .... 8 pts/model
- Big choppa ....+5 pts
- Big shoota ....+5 pts
- Killsaw (single/pair) ....+10 pts / +15 pts
- Kombi-weapon with rokkit launcha ..+10 pts
- Kombi-weapon with skorcha ....+15 pts
- Power klaw ....+10 pts
- Power stabba ....+5 pts
- Rokkit launcha ....+10 pts

Gretchin
Unit size .... 10-30 models
Unit cost .... 5 pts/model

ELITES

Burna Boyz
Unit size ....5-15 models
Unit cost .... 11 pts/model
- Big shoota ....+5 pts
- Kustom mega-blasta ....+10 pts
- Rokkit launcha ....+10 pts

Kommandos
Unit size ....5-15 models
Unit cost .... 9 pts/model
- Power klaw ....+10 pts

Mad Dok Grotsnik
Unit size .... 1 model
Unit cost .... 90 pts

Meganobz
Unit size ....3-10 models
Unit cost .... 25 pts/model
- Killsaw (single/pair) .... 10 pts / +15 pts
- Kombi-weapon with rokkit launcha ..+10 pts
- Kombi-weapon with skorcha ....+15 pts
- Kustom shoota ....+3 pts
- Power klaw ....+10 pts

Mek
Unit size .... 1 model
Unit cost .... 25 pts
- Grot Oiler ....+5 pts
- Killsaw ....+10 pts
- Kustom mega-slugga ....+5 pts

Nob with Waaagh! Banner
Unit size .... 1 model
Unit cost .... 85 pts
- Kustom shoota ....+3 pts
- Power klaw ....+10 pts

Nobz
Unit size ....5-10 models
Unit cost .... 17 pts/model
- Ammo Runt ....+5 pts
- Big choppa ....+5 pts
- Cybork body ....+5 pts
- Killsaw (single/pair) ....+10 pts / +15 pts
- Kombi-weapon with rokkit launcha ..+10 pts
- Kombi-weapon with skorcha ....+15 pts
- Power klaw ....+10 pts
- Power stabba ....+5 pts

Nobz on Warbikes
Unit size ....3-9 models
Unit cost .... 30 pts/model
- Big choppa ....+5 pts
- Killsaw ....+10 pts
- Power klaw ....+10 pts
- Power stabba ....+5 pts

Painboy
Unit size .... 1 model
Unit cost .... 65 pts

Runtherd
Unit size .... 1 model
Unit cost .... 40 pts

Tankbustas
Unit size ....5-15 models
Unit cost .... ? pts/model
- Bomb Squig ....+10 pts
- Pair of rokkit pistols ....+10 pts
- Rokkit launcha ....+10 pts
- Tankhammer ....+10 pts

FAST ATTACK

Boomdakka Snazzwagons
Unit size ....1-3 models
Unit cost .... 90 pts/model

Deffkoptas
Unit size .... 1-5 models
Unit cost .... 25 pts/model
- Kopta rokkits ....+25 pts
- Twin big shoota ....+10 pts

Kustom Boosta-blastas
Unit size ....1-3 models
Unit cost .... 90 pts/model

Megatrakk Scrapjets
Unit size ....1-3 models
Unit cost .... 110 pts/model

Rukkatrukk Squigbuggies
Unit size ....1-3 models
Unit cost .... 110 pts/model

Shokkjump Dragstas
Unit size ....1-3 models
Unit cost .... 110 pts/model

Stormboyz
Unit size ....5-30 models
Unit cost .... 12 pts/model
- Big choppa ....+5 pts
- Killsaw (single/pair) ....+10 pts / +15 pts
- Kombi-weapon with rokkit launcha ..+10 pts
- Kombi-weapon with skorcha ....+15 pts
- Power klaw ....+10 pts
- Power stabba ....+5 pts

Warbikers
Unit size .... 3-12 models
Unit cost .... 27 pts/model
- Big choppa ....+5 pts
- Killsaw (single/pair) ....+10 pts / +15 pts
- Kombi-weapon with rokkit launcha ..+10 pts
- Kombi-weapon with skorcha ....+15 pts
- Power klaw ....+10 pts
- Power stabba ....+5 pts

HEAVY SUPPORT

Battlewagon
Unit size .... 1 model
Unit cost .... 135 pts
- Big shoota ....+5 pts
- Deff rolla ....+20 pts
- Grabbin' klaw ....+5 pts
- Grot rigger ....+5 pts
- Kannon ....+15 pts
- Killkannon ....+15 pts
- Lobba ....+20 pts
- Stikkbomb chukka ....+5 pts
- Wreckin' ball ....+5 pts
- Zzap gun ....+15 pts

Bonebreaka
Unit size .... 1 model
Unit cost .... 180 pts
- Big shoota ....+5 pts
- Grabbin' klaw ....+5 pts
- Grot rigger ....+5 pts
- Kannon ....+15 pts
- Killkannon ....+15 pts
- Lobba ....+20 pts
- Stikkbomb chukka ....+5 pts
- Wreckin' ball ....+5 pts
- Zzap gun ....+15 pts

Deff Dreads
Unit size ....1-3 models
Unit cost .... 75 pts/model
- Dread klaw ....+10 pts
- Dread saw ....+5 pts
- Kustom mega-blasta ....+5 pts
- Rokkit launcha ....+5 pts
- Skorcha ....+10 pts

Flash Gitz
Unit size ....5-10 models
Unit cost .... 32 pts/model
- Ammo Runt ....+5 pts

Gorkanaut
Unit size .... 1 model
Unit cost .... 340 pts

Gunwagon
Unit size .... 1 model
Unit cost .... 175 pts
- Big shoota ....+5 pts
- Grabbin' klaw ....+5 pts
- Grot rigger ....+5 pts
- Lobba ....+20 pts
- Stikkbomb chukka ....+5 pts
- Wreckin' ball ....+5 pts

Killa Kans
Unit size .... 1-6 models
Unit cost .... 50 pts/model
- Grotzooka .... +5 pts
- Rokkit launcha .... +5 pts
- Skorcha .... +10 pts

Lootas
Unit size .... 5-15 models
Unit cost .... 20 pts/model
- Big shoota .... +5 pts
- Kustom mega-blasta .... +10 pts
- Rokkit launcha .... +10 pts

Mek Gunz (including krew)
Unit size .... 1-6 models
Unit cost .... 40 pts/model
- Bubblechukka .... +10 pts
- Kustom mega-kannon .... +25 pts
- Traktor kannon .... +10 pts

Morkanaut
Unit size .... 1 model
Unit cost .... 320 pts
- Kustom force field .... +20 pts

DEDICATED TRANSPORT

Trukk
Unit size .... 1 model
Unit cost .... 65 pts
- Grabbin' klaw .... +5 pts
- Stikkbomb chukka .... +5 pts
- Wreckin' ball .... +5 pts

FLYERS

Blitza-bommer
Unit size .... 1 model
Unit cost .... 155 pts

Burna-bommer
Unit size .... 1 model
Unit cost .... 155 pts
- Skorcha missiles .... +10 pts

Dakkajet
Unit size .... 1 model
Unit cost .... 110 pts
- Supa-shoota .... +10 pts

Wazbom Blastajet
Unit size .... 1 model
Unit cost .... 160 pts
- Kustom force field .... +20 pts
- Stikkbomb flinga .... +5 pts
- Supa-shoota .... +10 pts
- Tellyport mega-blasta .... +10 pts

LORDS OF WAR

Stompa
Unit size .... 1 model
Unit cost .... 900 pts

FORTIFICATION

Mekboy Workshop
Unit size .... 1 model
Unit cost .... 85 pts

T'AU EMPIRE
HQ

Aun'Shi
Unit size .... 1 model
Unit cost .... 55 pts

Aun'Va
Unit size .... 3 models
Unit cost .... 85 pts

Cadre Fireblade
Unit size .... 1 model
Unit cost .... 45 pts

Commander Farsight
Unit size .... 1 model
Unit cost .... 130 pts

Commander in XV8 Crisis Battlesuit
Unit size .... 1 model
Unit cost .... 90 pts
- Advanced targeting system .... +5 pts
- Airbursting fragmentation projector ..... +8 pts
- Burst cannon .... +8 pts
- Counterfire defence system .... +10 pts
- Cyclic ion blaster .... +18 pts
- Drone controller .... +5 pts
- Early warning override .... +5 pts
- Flamer .... +5 pts
- Fusion blaster .... +15 pts
- Missile pod .... +15 pts
- Multi-tracker .... +5 pts
- Plasma rifle .... +8 pts
- Shield generator .... +10 pts
- Target lock .... +5 pts
- Velocity tracker .... +5 pts
- XV8-02 Crisis Iridium Battlesuit .... +10 pts

Commander in XV85 Enforcer Battlesuit
Unit size .... 1 model
Unit cost .... 100 pts
- Advanced targeting system .... +5 pts
- Airbursting fragmentation projector ..... +8 pts
- Burst cannon .... +8 pts
- Counterfire defence system .... +10 pts
- Cyclic ion blaster .... +18 pts
- Drone controller .... +5 pts
- Early warning override .... +5 pts
- Flamer .... +5 pts
- Fusion blaster .... +15 pts
- Missile pod .... +15 pts
- Multi-tracker .... +5 pts
- Plasma rifle .... +8 pts
- Shield generator .... +10 pts
- Target lock .... +5 pts
- Velocity tracker .... +5 pts

Commander in XV86 Coldstar Battlesuit
Unit size .... 1 model
Unit cost .... 120 pts
- Advanced targeting system .... +5 pts
- Airbursting fragmentation projector ..... +8 pts
- Burst cannon .... +8 pts
- Counterfire defence system .... +10 pts
- Drone controller .... +5 pts
- Early warning override .... +5 pts
- Flamer .... +5 pts
- Fusion blaster .... +15 pts
- High-output burst cannon .... +15 pts
- Missile pod .... +15 pts
- Multi-tracker .... +5 pts
- Plasma rifle .... +8 pts
- Shield generator .... +10 pts
- Target lock .... +5 pts
- Velocity tracker .... +5 pts

Commander Shadowsun
Unit size .... 3 models
Unit cost .... 135 pts

Darkstrider
Unit size .... 1 model
Unit cost .... 60 pts

Ethereal
Unit size .... 1 model
Unit cost .... 55 pts
- Hover drone .... +5 pts

Longstrike
Unit size .... 1 model
Unit cost .... 185 pts
- Burst cannon .... +8 pts
- Ion cannon .... +5 pts
- Seeker missile .... +5 pts
- Smart missile system .... +15 pts

TROOPS

Breacher Team
Unit size .... 5-10 models
Unit cost .... 9 pts/model
- Markerlight .... +5 pts

This unit can also include:
DS8 Tactical Support Turret .... +15 pts

Kroot Carnivores
Unit size .... 10-20 models
Unit cost .... 6 pts/model

Strike Team

Unit size..5-12 models
Unit cost..9 pts/model
- Markerlight ....+5 pts

This unit can also include:
DS8 Tactical Support Turret....................+15 pts

ELITES

XV8 Crisis Battlesuits

Unit size..3-9 models
Unit cost..25 pts/model
- Advanced targeting system..................+5 pts
- Airbursting fragmentation projector.....+8 pts
- Burst cannon..+8 pts
- Counterfire defence system................+10 pts
- Cyclic ion blaster ....+18 pts
- Drone controller..+5 pts
- Early warning override ....+5 pts
- Flamer..+5 pts
- Fusion blaster...+15 pts
- Missile pod ....+15 pts
- Multi-tracker...+5 pts
- Plasma rifle..+8 pts
- Shield generator.......................................+5 pts
- Target lock...+5 pts
- Velocity tracker ....+5 pts
- XV8-02 Crisis Iridium Battlesuit........+10 pts

XV8 Crisis Bodyguards

Unit size..3-9 models
Unit cost..30 pts/model
- Advanced targeting system..................+5 pts
- Airbursting fragmentation projector.....+8 pts
- Burst cannon..+8 pts
- Counterfire defence system................+10 pts
- Cyclic ion blaster ....+18 pts
- Drone controller..+5 pts
- Early warning override ....+5 pts
- Flamer..+5 pts
- Fusion blaster...+15 pts
- Missile pod ....+15 pts
- Multi-tracker...+5 pts
- Plasma rifle..+8 pts
- Shield generator.......................................+5 pts
- Target lock...+5 pts
- Velocity tracker ....+5 pts
- XV8-02 Crisis Iridium Battlesuit........+10 pts

Firesight Marksman

Unit size..1 model
Unit cost...30 pts

XV95 Ghostkeel Battlesuit

Unit size..1 model
Unit cost..125 pts
- Advanced targeting system................+20 pts
- Burst cannon..+8 pts
- Counterfire defence system................+10 pts
- Drone controller..+5 pts
- Early warning override ....+10 pts
- Fusion blaster...+10 pts
- Fusion collider..+5 pts
- Multi-tracker...+5 pts
- Shield generator.......................................+5 pts
- Target lock...+10 pts
- Velocity tracker ....+10 pts

Krootox Riders

Unit size..1-3 models
Unit cost..28 pts/model

Kroot Shaper

Unit size..1 model
Unit cost...25 pts

XV104 Riptide Battlesuit

Unit size..1 model
Unit cost..260 pts
- Advanced targeting system................+20 pts
- Counterfire defence system................+10 pts
- Drone controller..+5 pts
- Early warning override ....+10 pts
- Fusion blaster..+7 pts
- Ion accelerator.......................................+15 pts
- Multi-tracker...+5 pts
- Smart missile system ....+7 pts
- Target lock...+10 pts
- Velocity tracker ....+10 pts

XV25 Stealth Battlesuits

Unit size..3-6 models
Unit cost..26 pts/model
- Advanced targeting system..................+5 pts
- Counterfire defence system................+10 pts
- Drone controller..+5 pts
- Early warning override ....+5 pts
- Fusion blaster..+7 pts
- Homing beacon..+20 pts
- Markerlight ....+5 pts
- Multi-tracker...+5 pts
- Shield generator.......................................+5 pts
- Target lock...+5 pts
- Velocity tracker ....+5 pts

FAST ATTACK

Kroot Hounds

Unit size..4-12 models
Unit cost..6 pts/model

Pathfinder Team

Unit size..5-10 models
Unit cost..11 pts/model
- Ion rifle..+5 pts
- Rail rifle..+10 pts

TX4 Piranhas

Unit size..1-5 models
Unit cost..43 pts/model
- Fusion blaster..+7 pts
- Seeker missile..+5 pts

Tactical Drones

Unit size..4-12 models
Unit cost..20 pts/model

Vespid Stingwings

Unit size..4-12 models
Unit cost..14 pts/model

HEAVY SUPPORT

XV88 Broadside Battlesuits

Unit size..1-3 models
Unit cost..70 pts/model
- Advanced targeting system..................+5 pts
- Counterfire defence system................+10 pts
- Drone controller..+5 pts
- Early warning override ....+5 pts
- High-yield missile pod ....+15 pts
- Multi-tracker...+5 pts
- Seeker missile..+5 pts
- Shield generator.....................................+10 pts
- Smart missile system ....+5 pts
- Target lock...+5 pts
- Velocity tracker ....+5 pts

TX7 Hammerhead Gunship

Unit size..1 model
Unit cost..140 pts
- Burst cannon..+8 pts
- Ion cannon...+5 pts
- Seeker missile..+5 pts
- Smart missile system ....+15 pts

TX78 Sky Ray Gunship

Unit size..1 model
Unit cost..130 pts
- Burst cannon..+8 pts
- Smart missile system ....+15 pts

MV71 Sniper Drones

Unit size..3-9 models
Unit cost..20 pts/model

DEDICATED TRANSPORT

TY7 Devilfish

Unit size..1 model
Unit cost..70 pts
- Seeker missile..+5 pts
- Smart missile system ....+10 pts

FLYERS

AX3 Razorshark Strike Fighter

Unit size..1 model
Unit cost..118 pts
- Missile pod ....+7 pts

AX39 Sun Shark Bomber

Unit size..1 model
Unit cost..110 pts
- Missile pod ....+15 pts

LORDS OF WAR

The Eight
Unit size..22 models
Unit cost.. 1250 pts

KV128 Stormsurge
Unit size... 1 model
Unit cost.. 335 pts
- Advanced targeting system.................+20 pts
- Airbursting fragmentation projector.....+3 pts
- Burst cannon..+3 pts
- Counterfire defence system..............+10 pts
- Drone controller..................................+5 pts
- Early warning override ....+10 pts
- Multi-tracker.......................................+5 pts
- Pulse driver cannon ....+10 pts
- Shield generator ....+30 pts
- Target lock ....+10 pts
- Velocity tracker ....+10 pts

FORTIFICATION

Tidewall Droneport
Unit size... 1 model
Unit cost..75 pts

Tidewall Gunrig
Unit size... 1 model
Unit cost.. 125 pts

Tidewall Shieldline
Unit size (Tidewall Shieldline)................. 1 model
Unit cost (Tidewall Shieldline)....................75 pts
Unit size (Tidewall Defence Platform)..0-1 model
Unit cost (Tidewall Defence Platform)........75 pts

DRONES*

MV33 Grav-inhibitor Drone
Unit size .... N/A
Unit cost..+10 pts

MV36 Guardian Drone
Unit size .... N/A
Unit cost..+10 pts

MV1 Gun Drone
Unit size .... N/A
Unit cost..+10 pts

MV17 Interceptor Drone
Unit size .... N/A
Unit cost..+15 pts

MV7 Marker Drone
Unit size .... N/A
Unit cost..+10 pts

MV8 Missile Drone
Unit size .... N/A
Unit cost..+20 pts

MV31 Pulse Accelerator Drone
Unit size .... N/A
Unit cost..+10 pts

MB3 Recon Drone
Unit size .... N/A
Unit cost..+15 pts

MV4 Shield Drone
Unit size .... N/A
Unit cost..+15 pts

MV52 Shield Drone
Unit size .... N/A
Unit cost..+15 pts

MV84 Shielded Missile Drone
Unit size .... N/A
Unit cost..+15 pts

MV5 Stealth Drone
Unit size .... N/A
Unit cost..+10 pts

Designer's Note: With the exception of named characters (e.g. Commander Shadowsun and The Eight), if a unit is accompanied by any Drones, that unit's points cost is increased by the amount shown in this section according to the Drones it is accompanied with. The points cost for named character units takes into account any Drones that accompany it.

TYRANIDS

HQ

Broodlord
Unit size..1 model
Unit cost.. 125 pts

Hive Tyrant
Unit size..1 model
Unit cost.. 155 pts
- Adrenal glands...................................+5 pts
- Deathspitter with slimer maggots.......+10 pts
- Devourer with brainleech worms ....+10 pts
- Heavy venom cannon ....+20 pts
- Lash whip and monstrous bonesword ....+10 pts
- Monstrous boneswords ....+20 pts
- Monstrous scything talons.................+10 pts
- Stranglethorn cannon.........................+15 pts
- Toxin sacs ....+5 pts
- Wings ....+30 pts

Neurothrope
Unit size..1 model
Unit cost..95 pts

Old One Eye
Unit size... 1 model
Unit cost.. 220 pts

The Swarmlord
Unit size... 1 model
Unit cost.. 240 pts

Tervigon
Unit size... 1 model
Unit cost.. 180 pts
- Adrenal glands...................................+5 pts
- Massive crushing claws.....................+20 pts
- Massive scything talons.....................+10 pts
- Toxin sacs ....+5 pts

Tyranid Prime
Unit size..1 model
Unit cost..75 pts
- Adrenal glands...................................+5 pts
- Boneswords ....+3 pts
- Deathspitter ....+6 pts
- Devourer..+4 pts
- Flesh hooks ....+3 pts
- Lash whip and bonesword ....+3 pts
- Rending claws ....+2 pts
- Spinefists..+2 pts
- Toxin sacs ....+5 pts

TROOPS

Genestealers
Unit size..5-20 models
Unit cost.....................................13 pts/model
- Extended carapace ....+2 pts
- Flesh hooks ....+3 pts
- Toxin sacs ....+5 pts

Hormagaunts

Unit size..10-30 models
Unit cost..6 pts/model
- Adrenal glands..+1 pt
- Toxin sacs...+2 pts

Ripper Swarms

Unit size..3-9 models
Unit cost..12 pts/model
- Spinemaws..+3 pts

Termagants

Unit size..10-30 model
Unit cost..5 pts/model
- Adrenal glands..+1 pt
- Devourer...+2 pts
- Toxin sacs...+1 pts

Tyranid Warriors

Unit size..3-9 models
Unit cost..17 pts/model
- Adrenal glands..+1 pt
- Barbed Strangler....................................+10 pts
- Boneswords...+3 pts
- Deathspitter..+6 pts
- Devourer...+4 pts
- Flesh hooks..+3 pts
- Lash whip and bonesword.....................+3 pts
- Rending claws..+2 pts
- Spinefists...+2 pts
- Toxin sacs...+5 pts
- Venom cannon.......................................+15 pts

ELITES

Deathleaper

Unit size...1 model
Unit cost..65 pts

Haruspex

Unit size...1 model
Unit cost..170 pts

Hive Guard

Unit size..3-6 models
Unit cost..35 pts/model
- Adrenal glands..+1 pt
- Impaler cannon......................................+10 pts
- Toxin sacs...+5 pts

Lictor

Unit size...1 model
Unit cost..37 pts

Maleceptor

Unit size...1 model
Unit cost..170 pts

Pyrovores

Unit size...1-3 model
Unit cost..28 pts/model

The Red Terror

Unit size...1 model
Unit cost..55 pts

Tyrant Guard

Unit size..3-6 models
Unit cost..38 pts/model
- Adrenal glands..+1 pt
- Crushing claws.......................................+10 pts
- Lash whip and bonesword.....................+3 pts
- Rending claws..+2 pts
- Toxin sacs...+5 pts

Venomthropes

Unit size..3-6 models
Unit cost..33 pts/model

Zoanthropes

Unit size..3-6 models
Unit cost..50 pts/model

FAST ATTACK

Gargoyles

Unit size..10-30 models
Unit cost..7 pts/model

Mucolid Spores

Unit size..1-3 models
Unit cost..22 pts/model

Raveners

Unit size..3-9 models
Unit cost..20 pts/model
- Deathspitter..+6 pts
- Devourer...+4 pts
- Rending claws..+2 pts
- Spinefists...+2 pts

Spore Mines

Unit size..3-9 models
Unit cost..10 pts/model

HEAVY SUPPORT

Biovores

Unit size..1-3 models
Unit cost..50 pts/model

Carnifexes

Unit size..1-3 models
Unit cost..80 pts/model
- Adrenal glands..+5 pts
- Bio-plasma...+10 pts
- Bone mace...+5 pts
- Chitin thorns..+5 pts
- Deathspitter with slimer maggots......+10 pts
- Devourer with brainleech worms.......+10 pts
- Enhanced senses...................................+10 pts
- Heavy venom cannon............................+20 pts
- Monstrous acid maw.............................+10 pts
- Monstrous crushing claws...................+15 pts
- Monstrous scything talons...................+10 pts
- Spine banks..+5 pts
- Spore cysts...+10 pts
- Stranglethorn cannon...........................+15 pts
- Thresher scythe..+5 pts
- Toxin sacs...+5 pts
- Tusks..+10 pts

Exocrine

Unit size...1 model
Unit cost..170 pts

Mawloc

Unit size...1 model
Unit cost..125 pts
- Adrenal glands..+5 pts
- Toxin sacs...+5 pts

Screamer-killers

Unit size..1-3 models
Unit cost..120 pts/model
- Adrenal glands..+5 pts
- Spore cysts...+10 pts
- Toxin sacs...+5 pts

Thornbacks

Unit size..1-3 models
Unit cost..80 pts/model
- Adrenal glands..+5 pts
- Chitin thorns..+5 pts
- Deathspitter with slimer maggots......+10 pts
- Devourer with brainleech worms.......+10 pts
- Monstrous scything talons...................+10 pts
- Spine banks..+5 pts
- Stranglethorn cannon...........................+15 pts
- Thresher scythe..+5 pts
- Toxin sacs...+5 pts

Toxicrene

Unit size...1 model
Unit cost..150 pts

Trygon

Unit size...1 model
Unit cost..150 pts
- Adrenal glands..+5 pts
- Toxin sacs...+10 pts

Trygon Prime

Unit size...1 model
Unit cost..175 pts
- Adrenal glands..+5 pts
- Toxin sacs...+10 pts

Tyrannofex

Unit size...1 model
Unit cost..170 pts
- Acid spray...+5 pts
- Adrenal glands..+5 pts
- Rupture cannon......................................+20 pts
- Toxin sacs...+5 pts

DEDICATED TRANSPORT

Tyrannocyte

Unit size...1 model
Unit cost..95 pts
- 5 Barbed stranglers..............................+20 pts
- 5 Venom cannons.................................+45 pts

FLYERS

Harpy
Unit size .... 1 model
Unit cost .... 155 pts
- Heavy venom cannon .... +5 pts

Hive Crone
Unit size .... 1 model
Unit cost .... 155 pts

FORTIFICATION

Sporocyst
Unit size .... 1 model
Unit cost .... 115 pts
- 5 Barbed stranglers .... +20 pts
- 5 Venom cannons .... +45 pts

GENESTEALER CULTS

HQ

Abominant
Unit size .... 1 model
Unit cost .... 110 pts

Acolyte Iconward
Unit size .... 1 model
Unit cost .... 60 pts

Jackal Alphus
Unit size .... 1 model
Unit cost .... 75 pts

Magus
Unit size .... 1 model
Unit cost .... 85 pts

This unit can also include up to 2 of the following:
Familiar .... 15 pts/model

Patriarch
Unit size .... 1 model
Unit cost .... 135 pts

This unit can also include up to 2 of the following:
Familiar .... 15 pts/model

Primus
Unit size .... 1 model
Unit cost .... 85 pts

TROOPS

Acolyte Hybrids
Unit size .... 5-20 models
Unit cost .... 8 pts/model
- Bonesword .... +5 pts
- Cult icon .... +10 pts
- Demolition charge .... +10 pts
- Hand flamer .... +3 pts
- Heavy rock cutter .... +10 pts
- Heavy rock drill .... +15 pts
- Heavy rock saw .... +10 pts
- Lash whip and bonesword .... +5 pts

Brood Brothers Infantry Squad
Unit size .... 10-20 models
Unit cost .... 6 pts/model
- Autocannon .... +10 pts
- Cult vox caster .... +5 pts
- Flamer .... +5 pts
- Grenade launcher .... +5 pts
- Heavy bolter .... +10 pts
- Lascannon .... +15 pts
- Missile launcher .... +15 pts
- Mortar .... +10 pts

Neophyte Hybrids
Unit size .... 10-20 models
Unit cost .... 6 pts/model
- Bolt pistol .... +2 pts
- Cult icon .... +10 pts
- Flamer .... +5 pts
- Grenade launcher .... +5 pts
- Heavy stubber .... +5 pts
- Mining laser .... +10 pts
- Power maul .... +5 pts
- Power pick .... +10 pts
- Seismic cannon .... +10 pts
- Web pistol .... +2 pts
- Webber .... +5 pts

ELITES

Aberrants
Unit size .... 5-10 models
Unit cost .... 30 pts/model
- Heavy improvised weapon .... +20 pts
- Heavy power hammer .... +5 pts

Biophagus
Unit size .... 1 model
Unit cost .... 40 pts

This unit can also include:
Alchemicus Familiar .... 15 pts

Clamavus
Unit size .... 1 model
Unit cost .... 60 pts

Hybrid Metamorphs
Unit size .... 5-10 models
Unit cost .... 11 pts/model
- Bonesword .... +5 pts
- Cult icon .... +10 pts
- Hand flamer .... +2 pts
- Metamorph claw .... +3 pts
- Metamorph talon .... +2 pts

Kelermorph
Unit size .... 1 model
Unit cost .... 80 pts

Locus
Unit size .... 1 model
Unit cost .... 45 pts

Nexos
Unit size .... 1 model
Unit cost .... 55 pts

Purestrain Genestealers
Unit size .... 5-20 models
Unit cost .... 15 pts/model

Sanctus
Unit size .... 1 model
Unit cost .... 60 pts
- Silencer sniper rifle .... +5 pts

FAST ATTACK

Achilles Ridgerunner

Unit size..1-3 models
Unit cost....................................70 pts/model
* Missile launcher.................................+5 pts

Atalan Jackals

Unit size.. 4-12 models
Unit cost..12 pts/model
* Bolt pistol...+2 pts
* Demolition charge .... +10 pts
* Grenade launcher............................+5 pts
* Power axe..+5 pts
* Power hammer ....+5 pts
* Power pick..................................... +10 pts

For every 4 Atalan Jackals and/or Atalan Leaders, this unit can include one of the following:

Wolfquad...25 pts/model
* Atalan incinerator .... +10 pts
* Mining laser.....................................+5 pts
* Power pick..................................... +10 pts

Cult Armoured Sentinels

Unit size..1-3 models
Unit cost....................................35 pts/model
* Autocannon................................... +10 pts
* Heavy flamer................................. +10 pts
* Hunter-killer missile ....+5 pts
* Lascannon .... +15 pts
* Missile launcher........................... +15 pts
* Plasma cannon.............................. +15 pts
* Sentinel chainsaw...........................+2 pts

Cult Scout Sentinels

Unit size..1-3 models
Unit cost....................................35 pts/model
* Autocannon................................... +10 pts
* Heavy flamer................................. +10 pts
* Hunter-killer missile ....+5 pts
* Lascannon .... +15 pts
* Missile launcher........................... +15 pts
* Sentinel chainsaw...........................+2 pts

HEAVY SUPPORT

Brood Brothers Heavy Weapons Squad

Unit size .... 3 models
Unit cost .... 50 pts
* Lascannon ....+5 pts
* Missile launcher...............................+5 pts

Cult Leman Russ

Unit size...1 model
Unit cost .... 140 pts
* Augur array ....+5 pts
* Battle cannon ....+5 pts
* Dozer blade ....+5 pts
* Exterminator autocannon .... +15 pts
* Heavy bolter................................... +15 pts
* Heavy flamer................................. +15 pts
* Heavy stubber...................................+5 pts
* Hunter-killer missile ....+5 pts
* Lascannon .... +20 pts
* Multi-melta .... +25 pts
* Plasma cannon.............................. +20 pts
* Storm bolter......................................+3 pts
* Track guards ....+5 pts
*

Goliath Rockgrinder

Unit size...1 model
Unit cost .... 95 pts
* Clearance incinerator .... +15 pts
* Cache of demolition charges.............. +10 pts

DEDICATED TRANSPORT

Cult Chimera

Unit size..1 model
Unit cost.. 65 pts
* Augur array ....+5 pts
* Dozer blade ....+5 pts
* Heavy bolter................................... +10 pts
* Heavy flamer................................. +10 pts
* Heavy stubber...................................+5 pts
* Hunter-killer missile ....+5 pts
* Storm bolter......................................+3 pts
* Track guards ....+5 pts

Goliath Truck

Unit size..1 model
Unit cost.. 75 pts
* Cache of demolition charges.............. +10 pts

FORTIFICATION

Tectonic Fragdrill

Unit size..1 model
Unit cost.. 80 pts

UNALIGNED FORTIFICATIONS

FORTIFICATION

Aegis Defence Line
Unit size...1 model
Unit cost..80 pts
- Icarus lascannon ....+20 pts
- Quad gun ....+30 pts

Chaos Bastion
Unit size...1 model
Unit cost..210 pts
- Icarus lascannon ....+20 pts
- Quad gun ....+30 pts

Firestorm Redoubt
Unit size...1 model
Unit cost..210 pts
- Punisher gatling cannon...................+15 pts
- Quad icarus lascannon ....+60 pts

Fortress of Redemption
Unit size...1 model
Unit cost..440 pts
- Heavy bolter.................................+15 pts

Imperial Bastion
Unit size...1 model
Unit cost..210 pts
- Icarus lascannon ....+20 pts
- Quad gun ....+30 pts

Imperial Bunker
Unit size...1 model
Unit cost..90 pts
- Icarus lascannon ....+20 pts
- Quad gun ....+30 pts

Imperial Defence Line
Unit size...1 model
Unit cost..90 pts

Macro-cannon Aquila Strongpoint
Unit size...1 model
Unit cost..440 pts
- Heavy bolter.................................+15 pts

Plasma Obliterator
Unit size...1 model
Unit cost..210 pts

Skyshield Landing Pad
Unit size...1 model
Unit cost..120 pts

Vengeance Weapon Batteries
Unit size..1-2 models
Unit cost.................................110 pts/model
- Punisher gatling cannon...................+15 pts
- Quad icarus lascannon ....+60 pts

Void Shield Generator
Unit size...1 model
Unit cost..200 pts

Vortex Missile Aquila Strongpoint
Unit size...1 model
Unit cost..470 pts
- Heavy bolter.................................+15 pts

FORGE WORLD POINTS VALUES

SPACE MARINES

HQ

Armenneus Valthex
Unit size .... 1 model
Unit cost .... 105 pts

Asterion Moloc
Unit size .... 1 model
Unit cost .... 170 pts

Bray'arth Ashmantle
Unit size .... 1 model
Unit cost .... 220 pts

Carab Culln the Risen
Unit size .... 1 model
Unit cost .... 265 pts

Casan Sabius
Unit size .... 1 model
Unit cost .... 145 pts

Damocles Command Rhino
Unit size .... 1 model
Unit cost .... 90 pts
• Hunter-killer missile .... +5 pts

Gabriel Angelos
Unit size .... 1 model
Unit cost .... 150 pts

Hecaton Aiakos
Unit size .... 1 model
Unit cost .... 160 pts

Ivanus Enkomi
Unit size .... 1 model
Unit cost .... 100 pts

Lugft Huron
Unit size .... 1 model
Unit cost .... 160 pts

Sevrin Loth
Unit size .... 1 model
Unit cost .... 135 pts

Tyberos the Red Wake
Unit size .... 1 model
Unit cost .... 160 pts

ELITES

Deredeo Dreadnought
Unit size .... 1 model
Unit cost .... 190 pts
• Aiolos missile launcher .... +20 pts
• Boreas air defence missiles .... +20 pts
• Hellfire plasma carronade .... +10 pts
• Volkite falconet battery .... +10 pts

Leviathan Dreadnought
Unit size .... 1 model
Unit cost .... 220 pts
• Cyclonic melta lance .... +20 pts
• Hunter-killer missile .... +5 pts
• Storm cannon .... +10 pts

Relic Contemptor Dreadnought
Unit size .... 1 model
Unit cost .... 140 pts
• Contemptor plasma blaster .... +5 pts
• Conversion beam cannon .... +5 pts
• Cyclone missile launcher .... +25 pts
• Dreadnought chainfist .... +5 pts
• Graviton blaster .... +5 pts
• Heavy flamer .... +5 pts
• Kheres-pattern assault cannon.......... +10 pts
• Multi-melta .... +10 pts
• Twin autocannon .... +15 pts
• Twin heavy bolter .... +15 pts
• Twin lascannon .... +25 pts
• Twin volkite culverin .... +5 pts

FAST ATTACK

Deathstorm Drop Pod
Unit size .... 1 model
Unit cost .... 120 pts
• Deathstorm missile array .... +10 pts

Javelin Attack Speeder
Unit size .... 1 model
Unit cost .... 125 pts
• Hunter-killer missile .... +5 pts
• Multi-melta .... +10 pts

Land Speeder Tempests
Unit size .... 1-3 models
Unit cost .... 115 pts/model

HEAVY SUPPORT

Land Raider Achilles
Unit size .... 1 model
Unit cost .... 300 pts
• Hunter-killer missile .... +5 pts
• Storm bolter....................................... +5 pts
• Twin multi-melta .... +20 pts

Land Raider Proteus
Unit size .... 1 model
Unit cost .... 235 pts
• Explorator augury web .... +15 pts
• Heavy armour .... +15 pts
• Hunter-killer missile .... +5 pts
• Multi-melta .... +15 pts
• Storm bolter....................................... +5 pts
• Twin heavy bolter .... +30 pts
• Twin heavy flamer .... +20 pts

Rapier Carrier
Unit size .... 1 model
Unit cost .... 75 pts
• Laser destroyer .... +35 pts
• Quad launcher .... +35 pts

Sicaran Arcus
Unit size .... 1 model
Unit cost .... 155 pts
• Heavy bolter...................................... +15 pts
• Hunter-killer missile .... +5 pts
• Lascannon .... +20 pts
• Storm bolter....................................... +5 pts

Sicaran Battle Tank
Unit size .... 1 model
Unit cost .... 165 pts
• Heavy bolter...................................... +15 pts
• Hunter-killer missile .... +5 pts
• Lascannon .... +20 pts
• Storm bolter....................................... +5 pts

Sicaran Omega
Unit size .... 1 model
Unit cost .... 175 pts
• Heavy bolter...................................... +15 pts
• Hunter-killer missile .... +5 pts
• Lascannon .... +20 pts
• Storm bolter....................................... +5 pts

Sicaran Punisher
Unit size...1 model
Unit cost.. 155 pts
- Heavy bolter .... +15 pts
- Hunter-killer missile .... +5 pts
- Lascannon .... +20 pts
- Storm bolter .... +5 pts

Sicaran Venator
Unit size...1 model
Unit cost.. 170 pts
- Heavy bolter .... +15 pts
- Hunter-killer missile .... +5 pts
- Lascannon .... +20 pts
- Storm bolter .... +5 pts

Vindicator Laser Destroyer
Unit size...1 model
Unit cost.. 175 pts
- Hunter-killer missile .... +5 pts

Whirlwind Scorpius
Unit size...1 model
Unit cost.. 170 pts
- Hunter-killer missile .... +5 pts
- Storm bolter .... +5 pts

DEDICATED TRANSPORTS

Dreadnought Drop Pod
Unit size...1 model
Unit cost.. 70 pts

Terrax-pattern Termite
Unit size...1 model
Unit cost.. 180 pts
- Twin volkite charger .... +5 pts

FLYERS

Fire Raptor Gunship
Unit size...1 model
Unit cost.. 340 pts
- Quad heavy bolter .... +30 pts
- Twin lascannon .... +10 pts

Storm Eagle Gunship
Unit size...1 model
Unit cost.. 335 pts
- Twin lascannon .... +10 pts
- Twin multi-melta .... +20 pts

Xiphon Interceptor
Unit size...1 model
Unit cost.. 235 pts

LORDS OF WAR

Astraeus
Unit size...1 model
Unit cost.. 675 pts
- Ironhail heavy stubber .... +5 pts
- Twin lascannon .... +30 pts

Cerberus
Unit size...1 model
Unit cost.. 400 pts
- Heavy bolter .... +15 pts
- Heavy flamer .... +15 pts
- Lascannon .... +20 pts
- Multi-melta .... +25 pts
- Storm bolter .... +5 pts

Falchion
Unit size...1 model
Unit cost.. 600 pts
- Heavy bolter .... +15 pts
- Heavy flamer .... +15 pts
- Laser destroyer .... +10 pts
- Multi-melta .... +25 pts
- Storm bolter .... +5 pts
- Twin heavy flamer .... +10 pts

Fellblade
Unit size...1 model
Unit cost.. 600 pts
- Heavy bolter .... +15 pts
- Heavy flamer .... +15 pts
- Laser destroyer .... +10 pts
- Multi-melta .... +25 pts
- Storm bolter .... +5 pts
- Twin heavy flamer .... +10 pts

Mastodon
Unit size...1 model
Unit cost.. 800 pts

Sokar-pattern Stormbird
Unit size...1 model
Unit cost.. 1000 pts

Spartan
Unit size...1 model
Unit cost.. 460 pts
- Heavy bolter .... +15 pts
- Heavy flamer .... +15 pts
- Multi-melta .... +25 pts
- Laser destroyer .... +10 pts
- Storm bolter .... +5 pts

Thunderhawk Gunship
Unit size...1 model
Unit cost.. 800 pts

Typhon
Unit size...1 model
Unit cost.. 350 pts
- Heavy bolter .... +15 pts
- Heavy flamer .... +15 pts
- Lascannon .... +20 pts
- Multi-melta .... +25 pts
- Storm bolter .... +5 pts

FORTIFICATIONS

Tarantula Sentry Battery
Unit size...1-3 models
Unit cost..40 pts/model
- Tarantula twin lascannon .... +10 pts

GREY KNIGHTS

HEAVY SUPPORT

Land Raider Banisher
Unit size...1 model
Unit cost.. 265 pts
- Hunter-killer missile .... +5 pts
- Multi-melta .... +20 pts
- Storm bolter .... +5 pts

FLYERS

Grey Knights Thunderhawk Gunship
Unit size...1 model
Unit cost.. 800 pts

ASTRA MILITARUM

HQ

Death Korps Marshall
Unit size...1 model
Unit cost...35 pts
- Plasma pistol...+5 pts

Death Rider Squadron Commander
Unit size...1 model
Unit cost...45 pts
- Plasma pistol...+5 pts

ELITES

Combat Engineer Squad
Unit size...5-10 models
Unit cost..
- Engineer/Engineer Watchmaster 8 pts/model
- Engineer Weapons Team...........25 pts/model

Death Rider Command Squadron
Unit size...4 models
Unit cost...85 pts

FAST ATTACK

Death Rider Squadron
Unit size...5-10 models
Unit cost..20 pts/model
- Plasma pistol...+5 pts

HEAVY SUPPORT

Armageddon-pattern Basilisks
Unit size...1-3 models
Unit cost..130 pts/model
- Heavy stubber...+5 pts
- Hunter-killer missile..............................+5 pts
- Storm bolter..+5 pts

Armageddon-pattern Medusas
Unit size...1-3 models
Unit cost..140 pts/model
- Heavy stubber...+5 pts
- Hunter-killer missile..............................+5 pts
- Storm bolter..+5 pts

Carnodon
Unit size...1 model
Unit cost...110 pts
- Carnodon twin lascannon...................+10 pts
- Hunter-killer missile..............................+5 pts
- Lascannon...+5 pts

Colossus Bombards
Unit size...1-3 models
Unit cost..150 pts/model
- Heavy stubber...+5 pts
- Hunter-killer missile..............................+5 pts
- Storm bolter..+5 pts

Cyclops Demolition Vehicle
Unit size...1 model
Unit cost...50 pts

Earthshaker Carriage Battery
Unit size...1-3 models
Unit cost..120 pts/model

Heavy Mortar Battery
Unit size...1-3 models
Unit cost..70 pts/model

Heavy Quad Launcher Battery
Unit size...1-3 models
Unit cost..90 pts/model

Malcador
Unit size...1 model
Unit cost...210 pts
- Heavy stubber...+5 pts
- Hunter-killer missile..............................+5 pts
- Lascannon...+5 pts
- Storm bolter..+5 pts

Malcador Annihilator
Unit size...1 model
Unit cost...230 pts
- Heavy stubber...+5 pts
- Hunter-killer missile..............................+5 pts
- Lascannon...+5 pts
- Storm bolter..+5 pts

Malcador Defender
Unit size...1 model
Unit cost...260 pts
- Heavy stubber...+5 pts
- Hunter-killer missile..............................+5 pts
- Lascannon...+5 pts
- Storm bolter..+5 pts

Malcador Infernus
Unit size...1 model
Unit cost...250 pts
- Autocannon..+15 pts
- Heavy bolter...+15 pts
- Heavy flamer...+15 pts
- Heavy stubber...+5 pts
- Hunter-killer missile..............................+5 pts
- Lascannon...+20 pts
- Storm bolter..+5 pts

Medusa Carriage Battery
Unit size...1-3 models
Unit cost..120 pts/model

Rapier Laser Destroyer Battery
Unit size...1-3 models
Unit cost..85 pts/model

Thunderers
Unit size...1-3 models
Unit cost..120 pts/model
- Heavy stubber...+5 pts
- Hunter-killer missile..............................+5 pts
- Storm bolter..+5 pts

Valdor Tank Hunter
Unit size...1 model
Unit cost...335 pts
- Heavy stubber...+5 pts
- Hunter-killer missile..............................+5 pts
- Lascannon...+5 pts
- Storm bolter..+5 pts

FLYERS

Arvus Lighter
Unit size...1 model
Unit cost...85 pts

Avenger Strike Fighter
Unit size...1 model
Unit cost...165 pts

Thunderbolt Heavy Fighter
Unit size...1 model
Unit cost...210 pts
- Thunderbolt hellstrike rack................+20 pts

Vendetta Gunship
Unit size...1 model
Unit cost...210 pts
- Heavy bolter...+15 pts

Voss-pattern Lightning
Unit size...1 model
Unit cost...130 pts
- Lightning hellstrike rack.....................+20 pts

Vulture Gunship
Unit size...1 model
Unit cost...180 pts
- Vulture gatling cannon........................+10 pts

DEDICATED TRANSPORTS

Hades Breaching Drill
Unit size...1 model
Unit cost...80 pts

Trojan Support Vehicle
Unit size...1 model
Unit cost...85 pts
- Hunter-killer missile..............................+5 pts

LORDS OF WAR

Crassus
Unit size .... 1 model
Unit cost .... 240 pts
- Heavy stubber .... +5 pts
- Storm bolter .... +5 pts

Macharius
Unit size .... 1 model
Unit cost .... 310 pts
- Heavy bolter .... +15 pts
- Heavy flamer .... +15 pts
- Heavy stubber .... +5 pts
- Hunter-killer missile .... +5 pts
- Storm bolter .... +5 pts

Macharius Vanquisher
Unit size .... 1 model
Unit cost .... 310 pts
- Heavy bolter .... +15 pts
- Heavy flamer .... +15 pts
- Heavy stubber .... +5 pts
- Hunter-killer missile .... +5 pts
- Storm bolter .... +5 pts

Macharius Vulcan
Unit size .... 1 model
Unit cost .... 340 pts
- Heavy bolter .... +15 pts
- Heavy flamer .... +15 pts
- Heavy stubber .... +5 pts
- Hunter-killer missile .... +5 pts
- Storm bolter .... +5 pts

Marauder Bomber
Unit size .... 1 model
Unit cost .... 320 pts

Marauder Destroyer
Unit size .... 1 model
Unit cost .... 350 pts
- Hellstrike missile rack .... +20 pts

Minotaur
Unit size .... 1 model
Unit cost .... 300 pts

Praetor
Unit size .... 1 model
Unit cost .... 400 pts
- Heavy stubber .... +5 pts
- Storm bolter .... +5 pts

Stormblade
Unit size .... 1 model
Unit cost .... 380 pts
- Heavy stubber .... +5 pts
- Hunter-killer missile .... +5 pts
- Stormblade twin heavy bolter .... +10 pts
- Storm bolter .... +5 pts
- Twin heavy flamer .... +10 pts

FORTIFICATIONS

Tarantula Battery
Unit size .... 1-3 models
Unit cost .... 40 pts/model
- Tarantula twin lascannon .... +10 pts

INQUISITION

HQ

Inquisitor Solomon Lok
Unit size .... 1 model
Unit cost .... 75 pts

Lord Inquisitor Hector Rex
Unit size .... 1 model
Unit cost .... 100 pts

ADEPTUS CUSTODES

TROOPS

Custodian Guard with Adrasite and Pyrithite Spears
Unit size .... 3-5 models
Unit cost .... 55 pts/model
- Misericordia .... +3 pts
- Pyrithite spear .... +5 pts

Sagittarum Custodians
Unit size .... 3-5 models
Unit cost .... 50 pts/model
- Misericordia .... +3 pts

ELITES

Aquilon Custodians
Unit size .... 3-6 models
Unit cost .... 75 pts/model
- Infernus firepike .... +10 pts
- Misericordia .... +3 pts
- Twin adrathic destructor .... +10 pts

Contemptor-Galatus Dreadnought
Unit size ....1 model
Unit cost .... 170 pts

Contemptor-Achillus Dreadnought
Unit size ....1 model
Unit cost .... 160 pts
- Infernus incinerator .... +10 pts
- Twin adrathic destructor .... +10 pts

FAST ATTACK

Agamatus Custodians
Unit size .... 3-6 models
Unit cost .... 95 pts/model
- Adrathic devastator .... +5 pts
- Misericordia .... +3 pts
- Twin las-pulser .... +15 pts

Pallas Grav-attack
Unit size ....1 model
Unit cost .... 95 pts/model

Venatari Custodians
Unit size .... 3-6 models
Unit cost .... 55 pts/model
- Misericordia .... +3 pts

HEAVY SUPPORT

Caladius Grav-tank
Unit size ....1 model
Unit cost .... 205 pts/model

Telemon Heavy Dreadnought
Unit size ....1 model
Unit cost .... 280 pts
- Arachnus storm cannon .... +15 pts

DEDICATED TRANSPORTS

Coronus Grav-carrier
Unit size ....1 model
Unit cost .... 250 pts/model

FLYERS

Orion Assault Dropship
Unit size ....1 model
Unit cost .... 500 pts

Ares Gunship
Unit size ....1 model
Unit cost .... 450 pts

ADEPTUS MECHANICUS

ELITES

Secutarii Hoplites
Unit size .... 5-10 models
Unit cost .... 10 pts/model
- Enhanced data-tether .... +5 pts
- Omnispex .... +5 pts

Secutarii Peltasts
Unit size .... 5-10 models
Unit cost .... 9 pts/model
- Arc maul .... +5 pts
- Enhanced data-tether .... +5 pts
- Omnispex .... +5 pts
- Power sword .... +5 pts
- Taser goad .... +5 pts

DEDICATED TRANSPORTS

Terrax-pattern Termite
Unit size ....1 model
Unit cost .... 180 pts
- Twin volkite charger .... +5 pts

IMPERIAL KNIGHTS

LORDS OF WAR

Acastus Knight Asterius
Unit size......................................1 model
Unit cost ....750 pts

Acastus Knight Porphyrion
Unit size......................................1 model
Unit cost ....780 pts
- Acastus lascannon ....+5 pts
- Helios defence missiles ....+10 pts

Cerastus Knight Acheron
Unit size......................................1 model
Unit cost ....480 pts

Cerastus Knight Atrapos
Unit size......................................1 model
Unit cost ....520 pts

Cerastus Knight Castigator
Unit size......................................1 model
Unit cost ....460 pts

Cerastus Knight Lancer
Unit size......................................1 model
Unit cost ....440 pts

Knight Moirax
Unit size..1-3
Unit cost ....155 pts/model
- Moirax conversion beam cannon.......+10 pts

Questoris Knight Magaera
Unit size......................................1 model
Unit cost ....480 pts

Questoris Knight Styrix
Unit size......................................1 model
Unit cost ....475 pts

TITAN LEGIONS

LORDS OF WAR

Warbringer Nemesis Titan
Unit size......................................1 model
Unit cost.......................................3800 pts

Reaver Titan
Unit size......................................1 model
Unit cost.......................................3000 pts

Warhound Titan
Unit size......................................1 model
Unit cost.......................................2000 pts

Warlord Titan
Unit size......................................1 model
Unit cost.......................................5500 pts

CHAOS SPACE MARINES

ELITES

Chaos Contemptor Dreadnought
Unit size .... 1 model
Unit cost .... 140 pts
- Conversion beam cannon .... +5 pts
- Graviton blaster .... +5 pts
- Heavy flamer .... +5 pts
- Hellforged cyclone missile launcher +25 pts
- Hellforged Dreadnought chainfist ... +5 pts
- Hellforged kheres-pattern
  assault cannon .... +10 pts
- Hellforged plasma blaster .... +5 pts
- Multi-melta .... +10 pts
- Twin heavy bolter .... +15 pts
- Twin hellforged autocannon .... +15 pts
- Twin lascannon .... +25 pts
- Twin volkite culverin .... +5 pts

Chaos Deredeo Dreadnought
Unit size .... 1 model
Unit cost .... 190 pts
- Aiolos missile launcher .... +20 pts
- Boreas air defence missiles .... +20 pts
- Hellfire plasma carronade .... +10 pts
- Volkite falconet battery .... +10 pts

Chaos Leviathan Dreadnought
Unit size .... 1 model
Unit cost .... 220 pts
- Cyclonic melta lance .... +20 pts
- Hellforged hunter-killer missile .... +5 pts
- Storm cannon .... +10 pts

Decimator
Unit size .... 1 model
Unit cost .... 160 pts
- Soulburner petard .... +10 pts

FAST ATTACK

Blood Slaughterer
Unit size .... 1 model
Unit cost .... 140 pts

Dreadclaw Drop Pod
Unit size .... 1 model
Unit cost .... 115 pts

Greater Blight Drone
Unit size .... 1 model
Unit cost .... 125 pts

HEAVY SUPPORT

Chaos Land Raider Achilles
Unit size .... 1 model
Unit cost .... 300 pts
- Combi-bolter .... +5 pts
- Hellforged hunter-killer missile .... +5 pts
- Twin multi-melta .... +20 pts

Chaos Land Raider Proteus
Unit size .... 1 model
Unit cost .... 235 pts
- Combi-bolter .... +5 pts
- Explorator augury web .... +15 pts
- Heavy armour .... +15 pts
- Hellforged hunter-killer missile .... +5 pts
- Multi-melta .... +15 pts
- Twin heavy bolter .... +30 pts
- Twin heavy flamer .... +20 pts

Chaos Rapier Carrier
Unit size .... 1 model
Unit cost .... 75 pts
- Laser destroyer .... +35 pts
- Quad launcher .... +35 pts

Chaos Sicaran Battle Tank
Unit size .... 1 model
Unit cost .... 165 pts
- Combi-bolter .... +5 pts
- Heavy bolter .... +15 pts
- Hellforged hunter-killer missile .... +5 pts
- Lascannon .... +20 pts

Chaos Sicaran Punisher
Unit size .... 1 model
Unit cost .... 155 pts
- Combi-bolter .... +5 pts
- Heavy bolter .... +15 pts
- Hellforged hunter-killer missile .... +5 pts
- Lascannon .... +20 pts

Chaos Sicaran Venator
Unit size .... 1 model
Unit cost .... 170 pts
- Combi-bolter .... +5 pts
- Heavy bolter .... +15 pts
- Hellforged hunter-killer missile .... +5 pts
- Lascannon .... +20 pts

Chaos Vindicator Laser Destroyer
Unit size .... 1 model
Unit cost .... 175 pts
- Hunter-killer missile .... +5 pts

Chaos Whirlwind Scorpius
Unit size .... 1 model
Unit cost .... 170 pts
- Combi-bolter .... +5 pts
- Hellforged hunter-killer missile .... +5 pts

DEDICATED TRANSPORTS

Chaos Terrax-pattern Termite
Unit size .... 1 model
Unit cost .... 180 pts
- Twin volkite charger .... +5 pts

FLYERS

Chaos Fire Raptor Gunship
Unit size .... 1 model
Unit cost .... 340 pts
- Quad heavy bolter .... +30 pts
- Twin lascannon .... +10 pts

Chaos Storm Eagle Gunship
Unit size .... 1 model
Unit cost .... 335 pts
- Storm Eagle multi-melta .... +20 pts
- Twin lascannon .... +10 pts

Chaos Xiphon Interceptor
Unit size .... 1 model
Unit cost .... 235 pts

Hell Blade
Unit size .... 1 model
Unit cost .... 135 pts

Hell Talon
Unit size .... 1 model
Unit cost .... 210 pts

LORDS OF WAR

Chaos Cerberus
Unit size .... 1 model
Unit cost .... 400 pts
- Combi-bolter .... +5 pts
- Heavy bolter .... +15 pts
- Heavy flamer .... +15 pts
- Lascannon .... +20 pts
- Multi-melta .... +25 pts

Chaos Falchion
Unit size .... 1 model
Unit cost .... 600 pts
- Combi-bolter .... +5 pts
- Heavy bolter .... +15 pts
- Heavy flamer .... +15 pts
- Laser Destroyer .... +10 pts
- Multi-melta .... +25 pts
- Twin heavy flamer .... +10 pts

Chaos Fellblade
Unit size .... 1 model
Unit cost .... 600 pts
- Combi-bolter .... +5 pts
- Heavy bolter .... +15 pts
- Heavy flamer .... +15 pts
- Laser Destroyer .... +10 pts
- Multi-melta .... +25 pts
- Twin heavy flamer .... +10 pts

Chaos Mastodon
Unit size .... 1 model
Unit cost .... 800 pts

Chaos Sokar-pattern Stormbird
Unit size .... 1 model
Unit cost .... 1000 pts

Chaos Spartan

Unit size...1 model
Unit cost...460 pts
- Combi-bolter.................................+5 pts
- Heavy bolter.................................+15 pts
- Heavy flamer.................................+15 pts
- Multi-melta...................................+25 pts
- Twin heavy flamer..........................+10 pts

Chaos Thunderhawk Gunship

Unit size...1 model
Unit cost...800 pts

Chaos Typhon

Unit size...1 model
Unit cost...350 pts
- Combi-bolter.................................+5 pts
- Heavy bolter.................................+15 pts
- Heavy flamer.................................+15 pts
- Lascannon.....................................+20 pts
- Multi-melta...................................+25 pts

Greater Brass Scorpion

Unit size...1 model
Unit cost...525 pts

Kharybdis Assault Claw

Unit size...1 model
Unit cost...400 pts

Kytan Ravager

Unit size...1 model
Unit cost...440 pts

DEATH GUARD

FAST ATTACK

Death Guard Greater Bloat Drone

Unit size...1 model
Unit cost...125 pts

CHAOS DAEMONS

HQ

Cor'bax Utterblight

Unit size...1 model
Unit cost...180 pts

Mamon Transfigured

Unit size...1 model
Unit cost...130 pts

Uraka the Warfiend

Unit size...1 model
Unit cost...145 pts

LORDS OF WAR

Aetaos'rau'keres

Unit size...1 model
Unit cost...700 pts

An'ggrath the Unbound

Unit size...1 model
Unit cost...550 pts

Scabeiathrax the Bloated

Unit size...1 model
Unit cost...475 pts

Zarakynel

Unit size...1 model
Unit cost...450 pts

CHAOS KNIGHTS

LORDS OF WAR

Chaos Acastus Knight Asterius

Unit size...1 model
Unit cost...750 pts

Chaos Acastus Knight Porphyrion

Unit size...1 model
Unit cost...780 pts
- Acastus lascannon........................+5 pts
- Helios defence missiles..................+10 pts

Chaos Cerastus Knight Acheron

Unit size...1 model
Unit cost...480 pts

Chaos Cerastus Knight Atrapos

Unit size...1 model
Unit cost...520 pts

Chaos Cerastus Knight Castigator

Unit size...1 model
Unit cost...460 pts

Chaos Cerastus Knight Lancer

Unit size...1 model
Unit cost...440 pts

Chaos Questoris Knight Magaera

Unit size...1 model
Unit cost...480 pts

Chaos Questoris Knight Styrix

Unit size...1 model
Unit cost...475 pts

War Dog Moirax

Unit size...1-3
Unit cost...155 pts/model
- Moirax conversion beam cannon......+10 pts

CHAOS TITAN LEGIONS

LORDS OF WAR

Chaos Warbringer Nemesis Titan	
Unit size	1 model
Unit cost	3800 pts

Chaos Warhound Titan	
Unit size	1 model
Unit cost	2000 pts

Chaos Reaver Titan	
Unit size	1 model
Unit cost	3000 pts

Chaos Warlord Titan	
Unit size	1 model
Unit cost	5500 pts

CRAFTWORLDS

HQ

Irillyth	
Unit size	1 model
Unit cost	140 pts

ELITES

Shadow Spectres	
Unit size	5-10 models
Unit cost	26 pts/model

FAST ATTACK

Hornet	
Unit size	1-3 models
Unit cost	80 pts/model
• Aeldari missile launcher	+10 pts
• Bright lance	+10 pts
• Hornet pulse laser	+5 pts
• Starcannon	+5 pts
• Crystal targeting matrix	+5 pts
• Spirit stones	+10 pts
• Star engines	+10 pts
• Vectored engines	+10 pts

HEAVY SUPPORT

Lynx	
Unit size	1 model
Unit cost	220 pts
• Aeldari missile launcher	+10 pts
• Bright lance	+10 pts
• Starcannon	+5 pts
• Crystal targeting matrix	+5 pts
• Spirit stones	+10 pts
• Star engines	+10 pts
• Vectored engines	+10 pts

Warp Hunter	
Unit size	1 model
Unit cost	195 pts
• Crystal targeting matrix	+5 pts
• Shuriken cannon	+10 pts
• Spirit stones	+10 pts
• Star engines	+10 pts
• Vectored engines	+10 pts

Wraithseer	
Unit size	1 model
Unit cost	130 pts
• Aeldari missile launcher	+20 pts
• Bright lance	+20 pts
• D-cannon	+40 pts
• Scatter laser	+10 pts
• Shuriken cannon	+10 pts
• Starcannon	+15 pts

FLYER

Nightwing	
Unit size	1 model
Unit cost	220 pts

LORDS OF WAR

Cobra	
Unit size	1 model
Unit cost	450 pts
• Aeldari missile launcher	+10 pts
• Bright lance	+10 pts
• Starcannon	+5 pts
• Crystal targeting matrix	+5 pts
• Spirit stones	+15 pts
• Star engines	+10 pts
• Vectored engines	+10 pts

Phantom Titan	
Unit size	1 model
Unit cost	3000 pts

Revenant Titan	
Unit size	1 model
Unit cost	1500 pts

Scorpion	
Unit size	1 model
Unit cost	500 pts
• Aeldari missile launcher	+10 pts
• Bright lance	+10 pts
• Starcannon	+5 pts
• Crystal targeting matrix	+5 pts
• Spirit stones	+15 pts
• Star engines	+10 pts
• Vectored engines	+10 pts

Skathach Wraithknight	
Unit size	1 model
Unit cost	325 pts
• Deathshroud cannon	+55 pts
• Inferno lance	+65 pts
• Scatter laser	+10 pts
• Scattershield	+15 pts
• Shuriken cannon	+10 pts
• Starcannon	+15 pts

DRUKHARI

HEAVY SUPPORT

Reaper
Unit size .... 1 model
Unit cost .... 170 pts

Tantalus
Unit size .... 1 model
Unit cost .... 310 pts

NECRONS

ELITES

Canoptek Tombstalker
Unit size .... 1 model
Unit cost .... 90 pts

FAST ATTACK

Canoptek Acanthrites
Unit size .... 3-6 models
Unit cost .... 40 pts/model

Canoptek Tomb Sentinel
Unit size .... 1 model
Unit cost .... 125 pts

HEAVY SUPPORT

Tesseract Ark
Unit size .... 1 model
Unit cost .... 170 pts
- Gauss cannon .... +15 pts
- Tesla cannon .... +10 pts

FLYER

Night Shroud
Unit size .... 1 model
Unit cost .... 190 pts

LORDS OF WAR

Gauss Pylon
Unit size .... 1 model
Unit cost .... 475 pts

Seraptek Heavy Construct
Unit size .... 1 model
Unit cost .... 650 pts

FORTIFICATIONS

Sentry Pylons
Unit size .... 1-3 models
Unit cost .... 100 pts/model
- Heat cannon .... +25 pts

ORKS

HQ

Warboss on Warbike
Unit size .... 1 model
Unit cost .... 115 pts

Mek Boss Buzzgob
Unit size .... 3 models
Unit cost .... 100 pts

FAST ATTACK

Grot Tanks
Unit size .... 4-8 models
Unit cost .... 35 pts/model
- Kustom mega-blasta .... +10 pts
- Rokkit launcha .... +10 pts
- Skorcha .... +10 pts

Grot Mega-tank
Unit size .... 1 model
Unit cost .... 90 pts
- Kustom mega-blasta .... +10 pts
- Rokkit launcha .... +10 pts
- Skorcha .... +5 pts

Nobz on Warbikes
Unit size .... 3-9 models
Unit cost .... 30 pts/model
- Big choppa .... +5 pts
- Killsaw (single) .... +10 pts
- Power klaw .... +10 pts
- Power stabba .... +5 pts

HEAVY SUPPORT

Kannonwagon
Unit size .... 1 model
Unit cost .... 170 pts

Mega Dread
Unit size .... 1 model
Unit cost .... 175 pts

Meka-dread
Unit size .... 1 model
Unit cost .... 165 pts

Squiggoth
Unit size .... 1 model
Unit cost .... 190 pts
- Kannon .... +15 pts

Big Trakk
Unit size .... 1 model
Unit cost .... 85 pts
- Kannon .... +15 pts
- Supa-kannon .... +50 pts

LORDS OF WAR

Gargantuan Squiggoth
Unit size .... 1 model
Unit cost .... 510 pts
- Kannon .... +15 pts
- Supa-kannon .... +40 pts

Kill Tank
Unit size .... 1 model
Unit cost .... 275 pts
- Bursta kannon .... +50 pts

Kustom Stompa
Unit size .... 1 model
Unit cost .... 800 pts
- Belly gun .... +50 pts
- Stompa klaw .... +20 pts

T'AU EMPIRE

HQ

Shas'o R'alai
Unit size .... 3 models
Unit cost .... 100 pts

ELITES

XV9 Hazard Battlesuits
Unit size .... 1-3 models
Unit cost .... 60 pts/model
- Fusion cascade .... +10 pts

FAST ATTACK

XV107 R'varna Battlesuit
Unit size .... 1 model
Unit cost .... 320 pts
- Advanced targeting system .... +20 pts
- Counterfire defence system .... +10 pts
- Drone controller .... +5 pts
- Early warning override .... +10 pts
- Multi-tracker .... +5 pts
- Shield generator .... +40 pts
- Target lock .... +10 pts
- Velocity tracker .... +10 pts

Tetras
Unit size .... 2-4 models
Unit cost .... 40 pts/model

XV109 Y'vahra Battlesuit
Unit size .... 1 model
Unit cost .... 300 pts
- Advanced targeting system .... +20 pts
- Counterfire defence system .... +10 pts
- Drone controller .... +5 pts
- Early warning override .... +10 pts
- Multi-tracker .... +5 pts
- Shield generator .... +40 pts
- Target lock .... +10 pts
- Velocity tracker .... +10 pts

FLYER

DX-6 Remora Stealth Drones
Unit size .... 1-4 models
Unit cost .... 60 pts/model

AX-5-2 Barracuda
Unit size .... 1 model
Unit cost .... 200 pts
- Cyclic ion blaster .... +10 pts
- Seeker missile .... +5 pts
- Swiftstrike burst cannon .... +35 pts
- Swiftstrike railgun .... +50 pts

Tiger Shark
Unit size .... 1 model
Unit cost .... 375 pts
- Seeker missile .... +5 pts
- Skyspear missile rack .... +25 pts
- Swiftstrike burst cannon .... +35 pts
- Swiftstrike railgun .... +50 pts

AX-1-0 Tiger Shark
Unit size .... 1 model
Unit cost .... 450 pts
- Seeker missile .... +5 pts

LORDS OF WAR

Manta
Unit size .... 1 model
Unit cost .... 2000 pts

KX139 Ta'unar Supremacy Armour
Unit size .... 1 model
Unit cost .... 1000 pts

TYRANIDS

HQ

Malanthrope
Unit size .... 1 model
Unit cost .... 150 pts

FAST ATTACK

Meiotic Spores
Unit size .... 3-6 models
Unit cost .... 20 pts/model

Sky Slasher Swarms
Unit size .... 3-9 models
Unit cost .... 15 pts/model
- Spinemaw .... +3 pts

Dimachaeron
Unit size .... 1 model
Unit cost .... 255 pts

HEAVY SUPPORT

Barbed Hierodule
Unit size .... 1 model
Unit cost .... 275 pts

Scythed Hierodule
Unit size .... 1 model
Unit cost .... 235 pts

Stone-crusher Carnifex
Unit size .... 1 model
Unit cost .... 105 pts
- Wrecker claws .... +10 pts

LORDS OF WAR

Harridan
Unit size .... 1 model
Unit cost .... 700 pts

Hierophant
Unit size .... 1 model
Unit cost .... 850 pts

MISCELLANEOUS

HQ

Aradia Madellan
Unit size .... 1 model
Unit cost .... 45 pts

Daedalosus
Unit size .... 1 model
Unit cost .... 55 pts

Elucia Vhane
Unit size .... 1 model
Unit cost .... 50 pts

Ephrael Stern and
Kyganil of the Bloody Tears
Unit size .... 2 models
Unit cost .... 125 pts

Janus Draik
Unit size .... 1 model
Unit cost .... 45 pts

Neyam Shai Murad
Unit size .... 1 model
Unit cost .... 55 pts

Obsidius Mallex
Unit size .... 1 model
Unit cost .... 130 pts

Taddeus the Purifier
Unit size .... 1 model
Unit cost .... 55 pts

Traitor Commissar
Unit size .... 1 model
Unit cost .... 55 pts

Valerian and Aleya
Unit size .... 2 models
Unit cost .... 200 pts

Vulgrar Thrice-Cursed
Unit size .... 1 model
Unit cost .... 70 pts

ELITES

Amallyn Shadowguide
Unit size .... 1 model
Unit cost .... 55 pts

Ambull
Unit size .... 1 model
Unit cost .... 75 pts

The Archivist
Unit size .... 1 model
Unit cost .... 90 pts

Borewyrm Infestations
Unit size .... 2 models
Unit cost .... 15 pts

Chaos Ogryn
Unit size .... 1 model
Unit cost .... 70 pts

Cultist Firebrand
Unit size .... 1 model
Unit cost .... 35 pts

Dahyak Grekh
Unit size .... 1 model
Unit cost .... 40 pts

Espern Locarno
Unit size .... 1 model
Unit cost .... 35 pts

Gotfret de Montbard
Unit size .... 1 model
Unit cost .... 40 pts

Guardian Drone
Unit size .... 1 model
Unit cost .... 90 pts

The Hullbreakers
Unit size .... 3 models
Unit cost .... 105 pts

Knosso Prond
Unit size .... 1 model
Unit cost .... 30 pts

Larsen van der Grauss
Unit size .... 1 model
Unit cost .... 25 pts

Negavolt Cultists
Unit size .... 4 models
Unit cost .... 50 pts

Pious Vorne
Unit size .... 1 model
Unit cost .... 30 pts

Rein and Raus
Unit size .... 2 models
Unit cost .... 40 pts

Rogue Psyker
Unit size .... 1 model
Unit cost .... 35 pts

Sanistasia Minst
Unit size .... 1 model
Unit cost .... 20 pts

UR-025
Unit size .... 1 model
Unit cost .... 45 pts

Ur-Ghul
Unit size .... 1 model
Unit cost .... 15 pts

X-101
Unit size .... 1 model
Unit cost .... 25 pts

TROOPS

Black Legionnaires
Unit size .... 2 models
Unit cost .... 28 pts

Chaos Beastmen
Unit size .... 4 models
Unit cost .... 25 pts

Cultists of the Abyss
Unit size .... 7 models
Unit cost .... 40 pts

Glitchlings
Unit size .... 4 models
Unit cost .... 20 pts

Nitsch's Squad
Unit size .... 6 models
Unit cost .... 40 pts

Spindle Drones
Unit size .... 4 models
Unit cost .... 65 pts

Traitor Guardsmen
Unit size .... 7 models
Unit cost .... 40 pts

The Vox-shamblers
Unit size .... 3 models
Unit cost .... 25 pts

FAST ATTACK

Cursemites
Unit size .... 4 models
Unit cost .... 20 pts

Eyestinger Swarms
Unit size .... 4 models
Unit cost .... 20 pts

Sludge-grubs
Unit size .... 4 models
Unit cost .... 20 pts